CONTEMPORARY INDIA AND ITS MODERNIZATION

BOOKS BY THE SAME AUTHOR

The Kamar
Indian Village
India's Changing Villages
Explanation and Management of Change

CONTEMPORARY INDIA AND ITS MODERNIZATION

S.C. Dube

VIKAS PUBLISHING HOUSE PVT LTD
DELHI BOMBAY BANGALORE KANPUR LONDON

VIKAS PUBLISHING HOUSE PVT LTD
5 Daryaganj, Ansari Road, Delhi 110006
Savoy Chambers, 5 Wallace Street, Bombay 400001
10 First Main Road, Gandhi Nagar, Bangalore 560009
80 Canning Road, Kanpur 208001
17-19 High Street, Harlesden, London NW 10

ISBN 0 7069 0288 2

Printed in India
At Delhi Printers, 21 Daryaganj, Ansari Road, Delhi 110006, and published by Mrs Sharda Chawla, Vikas Publishing House Pvt Ltd, 5 Daryaganj, Ansari Road, Delhi 110006

Preface

This volume brings together essays, addresses, and broadcasts focused on the theme of India's modernization. All pieces included in this collection, except the first, have been published in journals and anthologies. The lead essay, "Contemporary India and its Modernization," was sketched on 25 July 1973, my fifty-first birthday, and is previously unpublished. It is perhaps more critical than the others; it represents my frank reaction to the national situation as I see it developing in the twenty-sixth year of India's independence.

Several essays on interrelated themes, published in accessible symposia, are not included in this collection. The interested reader may also see "Cultural Problems in the Economic

Development of India" in *Religion and Progress in Modern Asia* edited by Robert N. Bellah (The Free Press, New York and Collier-Macmillan Limited, London, 1965); "A Note on Communication in Economic Development," and "Communication, Innovation and Planned Change in India" in *Communication and Change in Developing Countries* edited by Daniel Lerner and Wilber Schramm (East-West Center Press, Honolulu, 1963); and "Modernization and its Adaptive Demands on Indian Society" in *Papers on Sociology of Education in India* edited by M.S. Gore, I.P. Desai and Suma Chitnis (National Council of Educational Research and Training, Delhi, 1967).

Two younger sociologists, Yogesh Atal and Mukul Dube, are mainly responsible for this volume. Yogesh Atal persuaded me to bring out a collection of selected essays. At this point Mukul Dube took over. He used his discretion in selecting the essays and addresses, edited them, and saw the volume through the press. Besides taking care of repetitions, in editing he has made some stylistic changes, but my substantive arguments have been left intact. Even in a book on modernization I find myself constrained by tradition to thank either Yogesh or Mukul. Both understand the virtue of silence.

For secretarial assistance I am indebted to J.C. Kaushal, G.S. Sharma, and S.K. Arora.

November 1973 S.C. DUBE
Indian Institute of Advanced Study
Simla

Contents

ONE

Contemporary India and its Modernization

Large classes of our countrymen have been deliberately suppressed by us in the past and denied all opportunities of growth in the name of religion and ancient practice. All over India, we see today millions toiling in fields and factories and starving in spite of their toil. How can we rid these millions of their dire poverty and misery, and make them share in the freedom to come ? We hear of the service of the poor, and sometimes even the exaltation of the poor. And, by a little act of charity, or service, we imagine that our duty is done. Having reserved very magnanimously the kingdom of heaven for [the] poor, we take good care to keep the kingdom of earth for ourselves. Youth at least should be above this hypocrisy.

Poverty is not a good thing; it is not to be exalted or praised, but [is] an evil thing which must be fought and stamped out. The poor require no petty services from us or charity. They want to cease to be poor. That can only come by your changing a system which produces poverty and misery.

Jawaharlal Nehru (1928)[1]

...[the] main objective is obvious and it is to gain independence, not for the literate and the rich in India, but for the dumb millions.

I shall work for an India in which the poorest shall feel that it is their country, in whose making they have an effective voice, an India in which there shall be no high class and low class of people.

M. K. Gandhi (1947)[2]

The first twenty-five years of India's independence present a mixed record of achievements and failures. In retrospect, they reflect some puzzling aspects of the country's inherent strength and weakness.

Many prophets of gloom had grudgingly allowed the Indian nation a life span of not more than ten years. The country, they had prophesied, will never be able to consolidate itself: whatever semblance of unity it may have achieved, these pundits predicted, will be shattered by the clash of a variety of communal, regional, and other parochial interests. Happily, they proved wrong; wise and determined leadership attained for the country a measure of integration that was

[1] Quoted from Dorothy Norman (ed.), *Nehru: The First Sixty Years*, Asia Publishing House, Bombay, 1965, Vol. I, pp. 163-64.

[2] M. K. Gandhi, *India of My Dreams*, Navajivan, 1947, p. 6.

definitely more than territorial. Some sore and sensitive spots still remain, but they are being handled with imagination.

In regard to the viability of India's democratic polity, there were some serious misgivings even among those who wished the country well. Their pessimism was not entirely misplaced, but it is to the credit of the country that it has weathered several storms without succumbing to the non-democratic allurements that few developing countries have been able to resist. Two smooth successions of leadership and three wars—one leaving the bitter taste of defeat, another inconclusive and, therefore, neutral in its effects, and the third generating a somewhat unbalancing euphoria—besides recurrent crises, have tested the strength of the country's democratic polity. To many, it is a miracle that India has survived.

On the agricultural and industrial fronts the country's performance is not as poor as some of its critics—foreign as well as Indian—make it out. The doubling of agricultural production and laying of solid foundations for the country's industrial development in a quarter of a century are no mean achievements. India's record in these spheres is better than that of most of the Third World countries.

But these achievements, monumental as they are, cannot conceal the equally monumental failures. There appears to be a cruel irony in the predicament in which the country finds itself today: soon after demonstrating successfully its strength in a decisive victory on the Bangladesh issue and gaining worldwide recognition as a regional power of some consequence, the country has had a sobering reminder of its latent weakness. It is finding itself unable to stand the stresses and strains of its internal problems: its policy making and performance capabilities appear to be paralyzed. In the twenty-sixth year after the attainment of freedom—while the celebrations of the silver jubilee of its independence were still on, though in a low key in the later part of the year—a sense of despondency has overtaken the country. At this juncture one finds a deepening economic crisis, at least a partial paralysis of government's authority, and an unmistakable erosion of confidence in national institutions. Violence is on the increase. Public morality is at its lowest ebb. The system appears to be cracking.

The country will hopefully tide over the present crisis, but the deep-seated maladies that have surfaced in the present context are not likely to die out with the overcoming of present hardships. They represent a crisis of character. Manifest or latent, they pose a serious threat to all efforts at nation building and modernization. Where did things go wrong? Even after two decades of assiduous talk of development and four Five Year Plans, why have we to make the cheerless discovery that some of our gains are more apparent than real ?

With the wisdom of hindsight we now know that our plans had an elite bias and were patterned on a model that generated and sustained parasitism and high consumption. We committed the tragic error of equating *higher GNP* with *development* and the acquisition of some *superficial attributes of the affluent West* with *modernization.* In the process, a large section of our people suffered callous neglect; to repeat a cliche, the poor became poorer and suffered almost limitless degradation. The dumb millions, for whom Gandhi wanted to gain independence and whose cause was so eloquently espoused by Nehru as early as 1928, remained in the background. Poverty became a live political issue only after the great schism in the Congress, but to many who jumped on the

Indira bandwagon it was no more than a political gimmick. The formation and implementation of the poverty eradication programme, left largely to an insensitive and wooden bureaucracy, lacked imagination and spirit. Absence of adequate political support at appropriate levels made it a non-starter. On the other hand, "black" money was allowed to grow to such proportions that it could run a parallel economy with impunity. Today it exercises invisible controls over several sectors of national life and negates efforts at building a just society. It has polluted the entire value system and legitimized double think.

The various estimates of poverty in India make dismal reading. Defining the "poverty line" in terms of either a minimum monthly per capita expenditure of Rs 15 to 20 (at 1960-61 prices) or of a minimum calory requirement of 2,250 units, Ojha,[3] Bardhan[4], and Dandekar and Rath[5] find poverty either on the increase or constant at a high level. In 1960-61, according to Ojha, the poor constituted 51.8 per cent of the rural population; in 1967-68 this rose to 70 per cent. Bardhan's estimates of the rural poor are: 38 per cent in 1960-61, 44.6 per cent in 1964-65, and 53 per cent in 1967-68. Dandekar and Rath strike a slightly more encouraging note. According to them, poverty in the rural and urban areas has been constant over the years with 40 per cent of the population remaining below the poverty line. Minhas[6]

[3] P. D. Ojha, "A Configuration of Indian Poverty: Inequality and Level of Living," in *Reserve Bank of India Bulletin*, XXIV, 1, 1970, pp. 16-27.

[4] Pranab K. Bardhan, "On the Minimum Levels of Living and the Rural Poor," in *Indian Economic Review*, Vol. I, 1970, pp. 129-36.

[5] V. M Dandekar, and N. Rath, "Poverty in India," in *Economic and Political Weekly*, Vol. I & II, 1971.

[6] B. S. Minhas, "Rural Poverty, Land Distribution and Development Strategy," in *Indian Economic Review*, Vol. I, 1970, pp. 97-128.

estimates some decline in rural poverty from 52.4 per cent in 1956-57 to 46 per cent in 1960-61, 39.3 per cent in 1964-65, and 37.1 per cent in 1967-68. Even if we accept the estimates of Dandekar and Rath or of Minhas, the country has an enormous problem in the dimension of its rural and urban poverty.

The avenues to affluence have been monopolized by a small elite which has had it really good in the last twenty-five years. There has been a sizable increase in the number of those who live off the State in comfort and are for ever seeking more for themselves. These groups have set new standards of high consumption and ostentatious living, a trend that was criticized only in whispers but the irrevocability of which was conceded by the compliant and the indifferent majority. The critics of this segment are more vocal today and curiously some of the most ardent among them are those who have enjoyed and continue to enjoy all the privileges of the select elite.

Between the affluent (less than 5 per cent) and those below the poverty line (approximately 40 per cent) there is the nebulous middle class. This deceptive label hides more than it reveals. A sizable part of it is marginally above the poverty line, but its security is extremely precarious. This bottom level is in fact poor, though it suffers less degradation. Above it, in ascending order, are several levels enjoying progressively higher degrees of security. These groups are making desperate efforts to conform to traditional norms of middle class respectability, but soaring prices and mounting unemployment are making this increasingly difficult. The relatively well-to-do, i.e. the top level of this strata, has set its sights on the life styles of the affluent. The standards of the affluent are above its means, and efforts to emulate them lead to some pathetic results. Low resource, high living produces a series of psychological stresses and financial breakdowns.

The distributive aspects of economic growth and the diffusion of the benefits of modernization appear to have received little serious thought. If they have, neither policy nor performance reflects them adequately. *Development* that makes no visible change in the degraded lot of the common man—the majority in the country's population—is no development. Growth that permits a small segment of the society to wallow in vulgar high living is immoral. No country permitting sixty million children to remain undernourished can justifiably register the claim that it is modernizing. Then there is runaway unemployment. Fourteen million people are on the roster of the unemployed today. An estimate suggests that 8,000 persons are added to it every day. At this rate, in 1980, their number is likely to be thirty-seven million. Despite all efforts there is little evidence of our capability to arrest population explosion. Inflationary pressure is increasing and prices cannot be held in check.

Realization of these weaknesses is dawning, but we have rarely responded to the challenge by anything more than an expression of pious platitudes. Often the response is ritualistic. Brave postures are adopted and ambitious programmes announced, but beyond this not much happens. From ritual to retreat is easy. Non-action can always be rationalized.

Good intentions are certainly there, but not many can be translated into action. The leadership has to act through an apparatus—political and administrative—that shows every symptom of a moral collapse, and an enormous chasm separates profession from practice. In public we preach egalitarianism, but in private we continue to practise elitism; austerity is our proclaimed ideal, but consumerism is our cherished practice. Rampant corruption and nepotism are a product of the prevailing state of moral decay. The cancer has spread so extensively that the leadership does not know where to start combating it. The will to address ourselves constructively to the challenges is absent. The people are either apathetic and fatalistically accept the situation or reacting in anger indulge in senseless destruction. Both are counter-productive. The situation is grim, but it is not one without hope. But the longer we delay handling it resolutely the more it will get out of hand.

Modernization has been a prominent theme of investigation and debate in the last two decades. A wide variety of academic disciplines have joined together to resolve the many dilemmas of modernization. Significant historical, economic, psychological, political, and sociological perspectives have emerged on the subject. In fact this is one of the areas of social science inquiry in which a powerful inter-disciplinary thrust has been made.[7] Some of the major achievements of this scholarly endeavour are identification of the broad features of traditional and modern societies, preparation of a set of indicators of modernization, historical analyses of forces and factors leading to the modernization of different societies, critical and often perceptive comment on the causes of its breakdown, and a multi-disciplinary effort to determine its prerequisites. Some attention has been given to developing management guidelines to ensure rapid and, if possible,

[7] For a summary of some aspects of this discussion see S. C. Dube, *Explanation and Management of Change*, Tata McGraw-Hill Publishing Co. Ltd., Bombay-New Delhi, 1971, Chapters 3 and 4. Also, my article, "Modernisation and its Adaptive Demands on Indian Society," in *Papers on Sociology of Education in India*, edited by M. S. Gore, I. P. Desai and Suma Chitnis, National Council of Educational Research and Training, Delhi, 1967.

painless modernization, but no conspicuous gains have been registered so far in this sphere.

A modern society is a *rational* and *scientific* society—one endowed with the capability of increasingly substituting traditional sources of animate power with new sources of inanimate power to produce a variety of goods and to operate a range of services that substantially raise the level of the material well-being of the people. The attainment of this implicit objective is possible only through a series of complex formal organizations with highly specialized and differentiated role structures. Such organizations have to address themselves to the production and application of new knowledge as well as to the adaptation of knowledge available elsewhere, formulation and implementation of policy, and maintenance of adequate surveillance and control mechanisms. The effective functioning of these organizations presupposes a certain institutional and value framework which cannot be evolved without a series of characterological transformations.

The many impressive checklists of personality traits and societal attributes considered necessary for modernization represent useful scholarly exercises, but in operational terms they are not of much help. How does one build within the personality structure of the masses the attributes of rationality, empathy, mobility, participative impulse, achievement orientation, and faith in the desirability of change? New patterns of upbringing can certainly help. But how can we alter socialization mechanisms in a short time? The features of a social system characteristic of a modern society are well understood. There will be little disagreement that achievemental criteria should prevail over ascriptive ones, that the system of role relationship should be specific rather than diffuse, and universalistic rather than particularistic considerations should provide the normative basis for relations. But how are these transformations to be brought about? Many of these attributes and features are themselves the products of modernization.

Education and communication can be helpful in changing attitudes and values, but their capacity to do so should not be overrated. Sermons and exhortations often boomerang when the prevailing behaviour patterns are at variance with them. The answer to the problem appears to lie in radically altering the structure of economic opportunities and in introducing critical institutional changes. Initially traditional values may be an impediment to behaviour change, but if the incentives for the latter are strong behaviour does change and value changes often follow.

What is needed most is an adequate national framework for modernization. Several components of such a framework have been identified. First, the cohesive bonds of society must be strengthened. This can be done by encouraging consciously planned inter-regional and inter-ethnic interdependence, by secularizing political and economic participation, and by working for increasing acceptance of the legitimacy of the established authority. In this context, the close connnection between legitimacy and credibility must be emphasized; the latter is determined in a substantial measure by visible performance.

Second, social restraint and social discipline are important. These depend partly on the credibility of the established authority and partly on the latter's capacity to deal effectively with anomic trends of different types. Everyone, from the highest to the lowest, should be subjected equally to the norms of restraint and discipline. Differential application of these norms causes distrust and often leads to an ambivalent attitude to authority.

Third, the need for expertise, both in policy making and implementation, cannot be overemphasized. The administrative structure should be visualized as a series of interdependent and interpenetrating but specialized and differentiated roles. These considerations apply equally to the political sector.

Fourth, the reward system should be so structured that it encourages excellence of performance and curbs inefficiency and corruption. The canons of public morality should be applied with equal rigour to politicians, to bureaucrats, and in fact to everyone else.

Judged by these criteria, what has been India's performance during the last twenty-five years? There certainly has been a change in the structure of values and generally in the personality system, but this change is characterized by ambivalence both to tradition and to modernity. In point of fact, a new set of attitudes and values has been superimposed on the traditional value-attitude system. The two have not been integrated or synthesized. In any case a duality of norms is visible, resulting often in some bizarre manifestations of the simultaneous acceptance of both the old and the new. Education and mass communication have played their part in promoting new values, but it has to be borne in mind that apart from promoting new values they have been instrumental also in reinforcing some old values. Perhaps one should not look for any radical alteration in the value system of society as a whole, because the widening of economic opportunities has benefited only a few. A small section of India's population—the small elite and its satellites—which was more equipped to take advantage of the new opportunities and had the manipulative skills to make them more or less their preserve, profited from them. The steps towards institutional changes lacked imagination and boldness and were almost always half-hearted. The privileged class, though it paid lip service to the changes, invariably succeeded in watering them down to such an extent that these measures lost their thrust and failed to produce the results expected of them. Increasing politicization has enhanced the awareness of their rights in the general mass of the people and, in consequence, larger opportunities are being given to them now. The general picture, however, continues to be one of the twilight of transition: old values persist and new ones are being added to them.

Efforts to evolve a cohesive, stable, and durable nation have been more purposive, and have not received the credit they deserve. The territorial consolidation of the country was a considerable feat. The problems of social and emotional integration have also received careful attention. A sympathetic effort has been made to understand the genesis and implications of proto and sub-nationalism. The problems of the North-East Hill Areas have been tackled with great patience and in a pragmatic manner. Their problems may not have been solved to the entire satisfaction of all, but a stable solution is within sight. The secular approach to politics has also paid some dividends. One does not hear much about discontent among religious minorities other than the Muslims. The Muslims continue to have problems and national efforts to find a solution to them have not registered any conspicuous success. Deeply ingrained mutual suspicion and distrust hardened by separatist politics of the pre-independence era still persist. The situation has eased somewhat, but eruptions of communal violence do take place from time to time, and a section of Muslim leadership continues to follow a communal line in politics. Hindu communalism, though less militant, is still a force.

The greatest challenge to the cohesiveness of the nation is posed, however, by the slow erosion of the legitimacy of the established authority. The wide gap between policy and performance has considerably undermined the credibility of the government. This is a serious problem and needs to be given careful attention.

Beyond this point the picture becomes increasingly bleak. By slow stages norms of social restraint and responsibility have become so lax that today they appear to have lost all meaning. Myopic policies and poor performance partly account for this. We appear to have entered an era in which large sections of the people have rights but no responsibilities. An unfortunate impression has gained ground that even legitimate grievances are not redressed if attention to them is drawn in the normal democratic and peaceful manner. The payoff of agitation, pressure, and violence is much more substantial: small militant groups can hold society to ransom by adopting an aggressive posture. The government has lost its capacity to deal with anomic trends to such an extent that its threats to handle agitations and strikes with a firm hand, even with stringent penalties, are met by derisive laughter from those organizing them. As practical strategists the organizers of strikes know that persistence and pressure pay. And they do often get away with it. Pressure tactics are no longer confined to industrial and agricultural labour; they have also spread to elite segments such as pilots, engineers, and doctors—groups that are some of the best paid in the country. Even the guardians of law and order—the police—have taken to violent forms of pressure. Incredible as it may sound, even those responsible for directing the State function as if their political position has given them immunity from all restraint and social responsibility.

The policy processes of the country are in a state of total disarray for want of expertise. The generalist administrator persists in the make believe that given the opportunity he can rise to the occasion and no situation is beyond his capability. This is a myth that must be exploded. The academic sector has not given any better account of itself. Curiously it visualizes for itself only the role of a critic. It has offered little constructive cooperation in national development. In a country that has produced economic theoreticians of international renown, it is pathetic to find the Prime Minister making a vain search for a wizard who will guide her in taking the country out of its present economic impasse.

Notwithstanding several reviews of and probes into the administrative structure there has been no significant modification in the reward system. High capability, impressive performance, and general excellence rarely get the recognition they deserve either in monetary terms or in the form of allocation of higher responsibility. On the other hand, inefficiency and diverse forms of corruption are tolerated and sometimes even rewarded. That there is corruption in high places, also outside the public services, is well known. Corruption networks are functioning all over and are known to produce quick results. This corruption is rationalized in various ways, but it remains corruption nevertheless. The situation has become so intolerable that the normally neutral President of India lashed out at it in a public speech. The President's speech against the terrible decline in public morality may or may not have been an act of constitutional impropriety, but it certainly was an act of conscience and an act of courage.

Such a situation does not provide a propitious setting for effective programmes of modernization. The first necessity is that we should set our house in order. In the 1971 parliamentary elections the new programme of the ruling party had received massive endorsement from the electorate. Concrete programmes of its implementation have also not lacked support. Happily, there is an enlightened section of the elite which thinks more about society than about itself. There still is a sense of outrage in the people in the declining standards of morality and performance. If properly channelized this sense of outrage can be a national resource; left undirected today it is a wasteful exercise of impotent rage and senseless destruction.

The concept of modernization as it has been developed by its Western exponents is believed to be value free. It does make one important value assumption—the one regarding the necessity and the desirability of change. There is no standard model of modernization and no fixed path for its attainment. Developing societies can adopt a model of their choice and can chalk out their own path for its realization.

In India we have not spelled out the details of the model we would like to adopt for ourselves. Democracy, socialism and secularism have been adopted as the objectives of State policy, but no plan with careful specifications has been formulated. Strong overtones of ancestor worship have characterized our thinking, but no one has seriously recommended outright rejection of modern science and technology. Although there has been a great deal of talk regarding the desirability of achieving a synthesis between traditional Indian values and the values of modern science and technology, in formulating our policies we have made only a few nominal concessions to the past. All talk of socialism notwithstanding, the subconscious model motivating society is that of the high consumption societies of the West. Of course, several egalitarian alternatives have also been before us: the Russian and the Chinese models have attracted some, while the younger generation has been drawn to one or the other of the several different varieties of the ideology of the New Left. But consumerism has prevailed. It is time we remove the conceptual cobwebs and have a clear model of modernization.

The high consumption model of the West will not do for us as its injustice to a large section of society is too glaring. Even the United States, the world's most affluent society, has not been able to solve its problem of poverty. According to *Wall Street Journal*, in the super affluent economy of the U.S.A. one-fifth of the population is living in poverty. This is the situation in a society which has 6 per cent of the world population, but the economy of which uses 40 per cent of the world's raw materials. In any case, affluence has failed to solve several other social and cultural problems and has generated a variety of stresses. Frequent protests and strong dissent movements bear testimony to the younger generation's disenchantment with affluence.

Thus, we should work for a just and egalitarian society which will play down personal consumption and develop a variety of rich social services. The egalitarian model that we plan to evolve can draw from the experience of other societies—ranging from the Scandinavian countries to North Vietnam. But in the final analysis it must be based on a creative response to the realities of the Indian situation. No textbook can provide us the recipe that can meet all our needs. No animated discussion in the revolutionary jargon in well-furnished and airconditioned drawing rooms (or in more modest coffee houses) will produce a revolution. Rather than get lost in the whirlpool of unending argument, the intellectuals should come to grips with the Indian reality by developing organic links with the people. The ideology of "destruction first and development afterwards" addresses itself to only one of the challenges of modernization. A shift in the locus of power by itself will not bring about revolutionary changes in the quality of life. The less glamourous tasks of nation building involving sweat and toil will still have to the attended to. The cult of destruction cannot be taken too far. Obviously, we do not wish to begin with the Stone Age over again. Long ago Marx had indicated that the world cannot be anticipated dogmatically; a New World can be found only from a critique of the old. Revolution is a strategy, not magic. In a sense, it is the court of last resort.

In our quest for an appropriate model of modernization for India we shall have to project a workable utopia. The society we visualize for ourselves should ideally be a self-limiting society. It will have to give up the futile quest of "international standards" which are not quite relevant in our contemporary context. In any case we and the other countries of the Third World are not in a position to attain in the near future a per capita annual income of $2,400 which was the average for the developed countries in 1972. We shall, therefore have to define the social objectives and the cultural content of our model of modernization with the greatest possible care, laying emphasis not on the quantitative aspects of consumption but on the quality of social life. This theme is perhaps the most relevant for developing societies, but in respect of it little meaningful thinking has been done. In developing a "design for living" we shall have to take account of contemporary realities and also keep in view the consequences and desirability for the future of what we do. The established institutions of society will have to be subjected to a searching re-examination and limits will have to be set on trends that may jeopardize posterity.

Because of our rich and spiritual cultural heritage, we are exposed to an additional risk. Failure in adopting modern science and technology often leads to the short-sighted reaction of their rejection. In recent years the tormented youth of the West have been fed on ancient prejudices in the form of the gospel of nature. Thanks to the slick salesmanship of some of our maharishis, yogis, assorted godmen, and other vendors of spiritualism, practices and cults promising instant personal tranquillity and abiding solution of the sickness of civilization have become fashionable. With their new respectability gained in the West, it is likely that they may draw a section of our imitative society towards them and their modes of thinking. Such counter cultures can offer palliatives, not solutions. Let it be understood that answers to the problems of mankind can be found only through science, which is the only way to translate knowledge into rational action. Countering runaway technology is one thing, abandoning science is another. Science will have to be geared to definite social objectives, but it cannot be rejected.

In many ways the contemporary predicament of India can be attributed to certain global trends. There is a general increase in violence practically all over the world. Many governments are finding themselves unable to govern their citizens. Happenings in one country do not leave the others untouched. Mankind is failing in handling effectively the emerging problems of social organization. This does not mean that we should throw up our hands in despair and let our future be shaped by the march of events. Events can be controlled and directions for the future can be set.

The modernization of India has been caught up in rough weather. A number of factors that have contributed to the present stalemate were not of our creation, but no other country will bale us out of our present difficulties. At the same time we cannot disown the authorship of the unhappy chapter that is our living present.

TWO

Human Problems of Economic Development

The new nations of the world are undergoing today a second revolution. Most peoples and territories constituting the "underdeveloped" two-thirds of the world have already achieved the objective of their first revolution: their relentlessly fought battle for political sovereignty has been won. But, even before the joyful reverberations of political triumph could settle down, they had to plunge into the second revolution—a revolution aimed at bringing about an economic and technological transformation; a revolution intended to end the grinding poverty and the appallingly low standards of food, clothing, shelter, public health, and education. In terms of its human meaning, this second revolution is no less important than the first: the first brought to the people the form of freedom; the second is intended to bring to them its substance.

For the disturbed contemporary world this second revolution has a very special significance. It used to be said that one half of the world could not remain free while the other half was in bondage. Perhaps it can be said more aptly that one-third of the world cannot enjoy its prosperity in peace if two-thirds of it continue to be impoverished. The urge for freedom was motivated by the urge for a better life, and continued denial of basic human standards to the people of the new nations is likely to have most unsettling effects. It is necessary, therefore, to ensure that the revolution of rising expectations is not allowed to turn into a revolution of rising frustrations. This frustration can well throw the world into turmoil, and may even endanger civilization.

The urgency of the problem is now widely recognized. The concern for economic development and technological change is no longer the concern only of the underdeveloped nations. The advanced nations also are responding to the challenge. Today there is an upsurge of interest in the modernization of traditional societies. This upsurge is motivated partly by humanitarian considerations and partly, perhaps, by the anticipation of the possible consequences of the continuation of the present state of things. The vigour, determination, and dedication with which plans of economic development are being pursued augur well for the future of mankind.

The growing experience of national effort aimed at economic development and of international cooperation and assistance in planned change suggests that the problem is infinitely complex—one that cannot be solved only by good intentions or by wishful thinking. It has had a sobering influence on those who had faith in the magical ability of freedom to heal the wounds and cure the ills of a society kept in bondage. It has brought home the unmistakable realization that nation building cannot be done by exhortation alone, and that the process of economic development is not a simple and mechanical one involving only the provision of certain required inputs towards achieving, within a stipulated period, the desired objectives. It is now being increasingly recognized that there is no single approach that may be regarded as failure-proof. The task is immense and infinitely complex, and it requires a multi-faceted and multi-dimensional, a dynamic and variable, approach. In this context the critical significance of the human factor in the process of economic development has also been recognized.

Let us start with some general observations on the relationship between economic development and social change.

The process of economic development cannot be viewed independently of the process of social change. The two are inextricably interwoven and must proceed together. Within the arc set by its culture and social structure a society can absorb a limited number of technological innovations and can sustain the process of economic growth up to a degree, but it can soon reach a point when economic development will have to face insurmountable structural incompatibilities. If programmes of economic development do not anticipate accurately this structural opposition and conflict and do not plan well ahead to overcome them, they are likely to run into a dead end. It is essential, therefore, that an effort be made to build the necessary social infrastructures along with the purely economic infrastructures of development.

It is necessary to bear in mind an essential aspect of change. Man is teachable—he can learn to think and to act in new ways. The long story of his evolution suggests that he takes pride in being a maker, that he has consciously tried to build a better and a richer life for himself. But it must never be forgotten that his life cannot be manipulated beyond a point. Fundamental social change is a matter of a generation at least, if not of several. Age-old institutions and traditions cannot be done away with overnight. Impatience to usher in the New Order, however laudable, can lead to avoidable injuries.

It would be wrong to regard economic development as an end in itself. Its social purpose and cultural objectives should not be lost sight of. Economic development that does not lead to a richer and fuller life does not deserve much serious thought. It must have a sense of direction, a clear definition of aims. In this context we would do well to remember that, while economic motivation is undeniably important, it is by no means the only motivation. A model of development that takes into account only the economic incentive and the economic payoff is bound to prove inadequate. Developing a system of social incentives, rewards, and sanctions is equally necessary.

There is no single "model" of modernization. Nor is the process unilineal. No society can turn the wheel of history backwards to return to its past. Whatever the degree of idealization of one's cultural heritage, one cannot hypnotize oneself into returning to it. Modern problems need modern solutions. At the same time, one cannot reject one's history outright. That would be another kind of self-induced hypnotic state. It is curious how several elements of a people's history persist over time and how their symbolic function becomes an essential component of the self-image of the people. It would be an exercise in futility for developing societies to seek to adopt some hypothetical "techno-economic and socio-cultural" model of modernization: their values and institutions are bound to influence the course of modernization and will doubtless leave their impress on the emergent socio-cultural forms. At the same time, the ruthless logic of the compulsions of economic development will inevitably make several dents in the traditional structure, and it would be naive to assume that tradition can survive intact in the process of economic development and technological change.

This leads us to a related observation. A radical change in the economic order will involve an equally radical change in the social order. Individuals and groups alike are bound to feel the impact of these radical changes. All major changes involve some injury and considerable dislocation, and nations on the road to economic development must understand this. Careful planning supported by perceptive research can, however, help in making the process as painless as possible by minimizing the area of injury.

While change solves existing problems, it may also generate unanticipated ones. Wholesome economic trends can set in motion unwholesome social trends, and welcome social developments can lead to annoying economic consequences. The dilemma of social costs versus economic benefits constantly puzzles those who attempt a scientific analysis of the process of economic development. Even those who are not nostalgic about vanishing traditions have often to pause to wonder. Society has a way of reconciling itself to an emerging ethos: the secondary and tertiary effects of a new trend are perhaps not as painful as its initial impact. But it would be well to bear in mind that on-going economic and technological development recurrently generates new social problems. This need not persuade one to reject change, for it cannot be held in check, but it should certainly caution those who cherish the myth that economic development can solve all problems. The problems created by economic development are felt more by those countries that cannot or do not wish to divorce progress from considerations of social justice. They have, in some instances, to permit the retardation of economic growth in order to mitigate emerging problems that run counter to the canons of social justice adopted by them.

Before examining the human problems of economic development in a sociological perspective, let us outline briefly the contemporary situation in underdeveloped societies.

Viewing these societies from the economic angle, we find that they all have a low *per capita* income. Consequently, their level of savings is also low. This severely limits the possibility of investment from internal sources in projects of national development. Where a certain margin of savings does exist, it is always invested in items that are traditionally believed to offer security (such as gold and silver), prestige (such as giving impressive dowries or feasts), and salvation (such as building temples and shrines, and undertaking pilgrimages).

Most of these societies are primarily agricultural, and the level of agricultural and allied technologies in them is relatively low. They have a large subsistence sector, and the primary production sector dominates the economy. While there is no possibility of an appreciable increase in the land available for agriculture, the population dependent upon this land is growing in most countries. Agriculture has thus to employ large numbers who do not find any other economic outlet. This results in considerable disguised unemployment.

By and large, these societies are characterized by an ethos that is uninnovative and an ethic that is not entrepreneurial and industrial. This should not, however, be taken to imply that the traditional system does not have any "pockets" of modern economy. Such pockets exist, but their size is not large, and the traditional and the modern sectors are at best loosely integrated. It may be added that the industrial sector is dominated by the trader-producer, who lacks an industrial ethic.

The social configuration of these societies is not easy to delineate. Most of them have an "ascribed" status system. A person is born into a more or less rigidly defined status which inhibits his mobility and possibilities of achievement. Occupations and work-roles are, to a large degree, status-linked. Relationships—social as well as economic—tend to be of a personalized order: they are "particularistic" rather than "universalistic". Economic roles are not sharply distinguished from other social roles; the various roles often merge and get blurred.

Family and kin (or such larger extensions of kin groups as caste) claim the major portion of one's loyalty in these societies. The level of interest articulation is rather low and, as such, other interest-oriented and functionally specific associations are poorly developed. Traditional claims of family and kin regulate the system of distribution. Groups rather than individuals—or, at any rate, individuals representing groups—control resources and related decision making processes. The nation is often a series of autonomous communities that are at best loosely integrated into the wider national unit. Parochial—tribal, ethnic, religious, regional, and linguistic—loyalties assert themselves repeatedly and weaken the cohesive bonds of the nation.

Another important feature of these societies is their cultural emphasis on the sacred. The simple faith of men in these societies may be touching, but it often comes in the way of their being able to compute strategies on a secular ends-means level. Ritual considerations sometimes tend to dominate major economic decisions.

The psychological consequences of such an economic and social order are obvious. In such a milieu the people naturally develop certain characteristic attitudes and values which, in their turn, sustain the order. The precarious economic balance gives rise to fatalism. The individual's socialization, within the framework of a rigid status system and under the almost total control of the family and kin group, restricts mobility as well as situational and motivational choice. Recruitment to new roles is thus not encouraged. A closed system permits neither high achievement motivation nor the computing of strategies on a broad stage. The universe of action and choice making is thus necessarily restricted. The particularistic and diffused system of expectations and obligations blocks the development of "empathy", which is an essential requirement of man in a modernizing society. But these are all transitional societies, moving slowly from tradition to modernity. This movement is not a matter of choice and not entirely voluntary either. Compulsions of the emerging economic and political order perhaps leave them with no alternative.

In respect both of the ends and of the means of change, developing societies are somewhat uncertain and hesitant. They appear to have blurred images and conflicting goals. Standing in the twilight of tradition and modernity, these societies find the pull of the past powerful, but the compulsions inherent in the emerging social, economic, and political processes force them to take a few halting but nevertheless unmistakable steps in the direction of modernization. A large section of these societies clings to the precarious security that is offered by the traditional system—although its inadequacies are becoming increasingly obvious. The new future promised by the modernizing elite also attracts it, but this appears somehow distant and remote. The hard work and sustained sacrifice that it involves add to its remoteness. In any case a large number of people cannot visualize such a future in its broadest sweep and farthest reach. This contradiction between the elite formulation of the goals of change and the mass preparedness to adopt them merits notice. The absence of proper communication between the modernizing elite and the masses results in poor articulation both of the proximate and of the ultimate goals of change.

Another equally significant contradiction is the one found between the elite's aim of rapid transformation and the structural immobility of the masses. The social and economic infrastructures that are a prerequisite to economic growth do not exist in most of the underdeveloped societies. How the hopeful planners expect to gear the traditional system to the needs and the requirements of economic and technological modernization is a secret they have not chosen to share with others. It is only now that some belated recognition has been given to the otherwise imperative need for inputs in essential social overheads. It is sad, but nevertheless true, that in any curtailment of developmental expenditure, education and communications are invariably the first casualties. One wonders how a society can be modernized without any conscious and sustained effort towards the modernization of the minds of its members.

A third set of contradictions is presented by the elite itself.

In the overt formulation of the aims and means of change the different segments of this group perhaps agree, but only superficially. The conservative elite is not the only one to have a vested interest in the maintenance of tradition; certain sections of the so-called progressive elite are equally concerned about its preservation, not for reasons of nostalgia but for reasons of plain economic and political gain. In fact, the contradictions between their declared aims and their undeclared intentions are too glaring to be missed. Note also the contradictions between the aims and approach of the political elite on the one hand, and of the bureaucratic elite on the other.

One can go on adding to the list of these contradictions, but we shall mention only one more. This is the contradiction between the declared ideal and the actual practice in respect of the methods of bringing about change. All too readily, some countries allow democratic methods to be perverted into not-so-democratic pressures. Alternatively, the translation of democracy is left to either a wooden, unimaginative, and smug bureaucracy or to a power hungry and self-aggrandizing activist party. Even when some faltering steps are taken in the direction of institution building, the tendency is to deny the substance of power to these institutions and, thus, to stifle their initiative by rigid bureaucratic controls. The little power that is eventually transferred to them is hedged in by so many safeguards and controls that it soon ceases to have any meaning.

The presence of such cultural, economic, social, and political contradictions has important consequences for the success of the plans of economic development in underdeveloped societies.

The terms "traditional" and "transitional" have been

used here to denote ideal types. In point of fact no society is completely stable; the forces of normal opposition within its framework necessitate constant adjustments and alterations. In this sense any society at any given point of time may be regarded as a transitional society. However, we are concerned here not with normal evolutionary modifications and adjustments, but with fundamental changes in the social and economic order—with radical alterations that will make a qualitative difference in the structure and values of society. Such radical changes are intended in the underdeveloped societies. On the national level the urge to change appears to be motivated by the desire for respectability, for stability, and for power.

The Western impact—at least on the elite mind—has been deep and powerful. The "hated imperialist" has wound up and liquidated his empire but, while quitting, has left behind some significant ideas and images of modernization. His ways were rejected while he was in, but they are being imitated when he is out. The acquisition of certain elements of Western science and technology adds to the respectability—and the international acceptability—of an underdeveloped nation. To take a somewhat odd example, this search for respectability motivates even small and underdeveloped countries to start costly and uneconomic ventures in international aviation. Pressing needs of the people are bypassed to make heavy investments in glittering luxury jets. The same is true of television and tanks. It may one day become true also of nuclear weapons, unless this mad pursuit is halted by an awakened conscience. The adoption of certain other Western modes and styles, such as dress and dancing, is perhaps similarly motivated. There is no doubt that acceptance of Western traits and technologies confers prestige.

The second factor, stability, is perhaps more important as a motivation for the adoption of a policy of change by the underdeveloped countries. The national struggles for freedom against Western domination were built around certain promises—the promises of plenty and prosperity. The advent of freedom has witnessed a rising tide of expectations. The people are getting impatient, even restive; they are no longer satisfied with promises: they want performance and results. It is realized that old tools and techniques are no longer adequate for the fulfilment of these promises. Planned economic development through the adoption of science and modern technology seems to be the only way left for these countries to maintain their peace and stability. In the alternative, they are likely to be engulfed by a rising tide of frustration which can take many ugly forms.

The power theme also motivates many underdeveloped countries and leads them to adopt certain forms of change. Armed strength cannot be built without economic strength. These countries, therefore, take up programmes of economic development. The growing economic resources, however, are not ploughed back into fields where they would consolidate the economic position and would lead to continuous and sustained economic growth. A major part of the enlarged resources is invested in building military strength. The consequences of such a trend are not only unfortunate for the country itself but are unwholesome internationally, for they set in motion a chain reaction. Even if such countries do not adopt an aggressive posture because of their added strength, they do alarm their neighbours into following their not-so-creditable example. However unwelcome, this motivation for change is also much in evidence in the underdeveloped world.

National considerations and policies apart, the urge to change is found in individuals and groups also. Most often they change in response to the pressure of needs—felt, perceived, or induced. Ecological and demographic compulsions are known to have forced societies to innovate and to change. Contemporary social, economic, and political compulsions also necessitate a degree of change. It is not implied that man changes only when he is compelled to change. He also loves to experiment and to vary forms and techniques. All structural elements of his society and modes of his culture are not sacrosanct or even inviolable; there are certain aspects in which he is free to experiment and change for the sake of variation alone. And we should not underrate the role of choice in human behaviour. The choice of alternative forms may be dictated by the desire to imitate some reference group —a group that provides a "prestige model" or a "success model". Such a choice may also be made on the rational grounds of greater economy, efficiency, or ease of mastery. A change prone elite can help in enlarging the margin of choice by setting up an effective want-inducing apparatus.

Incentives to change are greater in societies whose orientation to change is not unduly restrictive. All cultures have "change prone" areas, but the general ethos of some is more favourable to change than that of others. Expectancy of change predisposes individuals and groups to adopt innovations more readily. Marginal individuals and "subordinated groups" are perhaps more change prone. Immediate economic and psychic rewards are among the most potent motivations for change. "Investment in the future" is a good and a necessary slogan, but it is human nature to desire some short-term benefits also.

The process of planned change is never smooth. A

modernizer must be prepared to face obstacles and to overcome barriers. He should anticipate them well in advance. The more obvious barriers to change are easily identified, and we need not go into their details. Some innovations are rejected because they involve changes in the established motor habits of people. Some do not find favour because they go against the tastes and the preferences of people; even logic and science cannot persuade people to give up some of their core beliefs and values. Some cannot be adopted because the social and psychological penalties that they involve outweigh their advantages. Many items fail to gain acceptance simply because the people do not have the economic resources and the educational equipment to adopt them. Finally, many innovations do not evoke a favourable response because their virtues are not convincingly explained to the people.

But it is necessary to go beneath the surface to identify the intangible human factors that influence the acceptance of change. Latent structural, ideological, and motivational incompatibilities often hinder the adoption of change. Some of these have been discussed earlier: an ascriptive status system of interpersonal relationships, a diffused system of expectations and rewards, kin-orientation, and sacred emphases, and the attendant social and psychological consequences of each. The wide cultural ramifications of these attributes often act as intangible barriers to change. A limited and constricted universe, the absence of achievement motivation and achievement opportunities, and the inhibited stipulation of strategies provide disincentives to change. Uncertainty regarding consequences and a fear of linked change are other significant disincentives.

We shall discuss briefly two basic questions —why do many of the programmes of planned change fail? In what manner and in what measure does the human factor account for their failure? Limitations of space do not permit a full-scale discussion of the factors responsible for the very restricted success of the programmes of planned change in many of the underdeveloped nations, but we shall summarily touch upon those that appear to be the most significant.

Many projects of development fail because they are based on inadequate and unrealistic identification of needs. The elite often projects into them its bias—ideological, economic, and political—beyond the point of feasibility. Rewards are sometimes so distant that they fail to enthuse the people, who do not find in the development projects any relevance to their individual, group, local, and regional contexts and needs. It would be futile to expect them to work endlessly for an abstraction such as the nation or the future without any immediate reward in view.

The choice of the agency or agencies to implement the plans also leaves much to be desired. Bureaucracy generally resists attempts to introduce changes in its structure and its methods of work, and does not yield easily to programmes of orientation and training. Thus, we get the paradox of civil servants oriented to law and order trying to run a social welfare administration. The bureaucrat can learn to cringe before the fumbling but domineering politician. He refuses, however, to develop even overt respect for the opinions of the common people. Smug and complacent, the bureaucracy blunders along. It is convinced of its wisdom and its infallibility and is contemptuous of any suggestions or moves to reform its ways. Politicians cannot easily free themselves from power considerations, and under their influence the political factor often enters into the choice of the local agents of change. If recourse is taken to institution building for developmental tasks, sound theoretical approaches in regard to them are vitiated by bureaucratic and political interference. The choice of an appropriate agency, the recruitment of the right kind of people for it, and the inculcation of the proper attitudes and skills in them perhaps hold the key to the success of programmes of planned change.

The actual strategy of planning and implementation is also lopsided and lacks balance. Priorities set for different spheres often do not fit together. Ideological excesses and elite biases are evident in them; they even reflect contradictory pressures and opposite pulls. And they often lack a sense of timing. The results can easily be anticipated: development projects pulling in opposite directions weaken each other or undo one another's beneficial effects. Ill-timed projects, however well-intentioned, are weak from their very inception. Communication can be a powerful instrument of economic development, but its full potentialities are rarely utilized. Exhortation has a place in the strategy of communication, but by itself it can achieve little. The communications media are not fully utilized to create awareness and interest and to inculcate attitudes and skills necessary for economic development. Encumbered by an urban-biased and sophisticated style, they rarely succeed in carrying their message to the people. Little effort appears to have been made to create a corps of media production experts who understand the mass mind and its cultural frame of reference, and produce messages in an idiom that can be readily grasped by the common man. No imaginative efforts are made to gear the traditional networks of communication to projects of nation building.

The planner and his action agents often fail to evaluate emerging social processes and their implications for the process of planned change. Their assessment of the cultural lags is also faulty. In consequence, they cannot suitably adjust and modify their strategies of change.

It has been suggested earlier that several types of incompatibilities come in the way of planned change. These are not difficult to identify. But a surprising aspect of the process of planned development is that those who control it are either unable or unwilling to do anything about removing them. Increased agricultural production is desired by the planner, but he does not act quickly and firmly enough to introduce land reform legislation to facilitate agricultural improvement. Many examples of this type can be cited to prove that there is great hesitation in providing the proper economic, social, and psychological base for the process of economic development to take firm root.

Then there is the undue hurry and impatience for results. The desire is understandable, but it sometimes leads to such frequent policy changes that gains from the projects cannot be consolidated. Often the course of action is altered even before the results of earlier efforts are manifested partially.

Finally, the failures of science and technology must also be considered seriously. Modern science and technology are not failure proof and, in specific contexts, they may not be readily adaptable. For a variety of reasons, the agents of change sometimes try to promote an inferior science and an inefficient technology. Alternatively, the science and the technology sought to be promoted may not suit local conditions. The conservatism of a people on a subsistence level is understandable. They stick to proven remedies of limited potency until the efficiency of the alternative is firmly established. And, of course, in terms of cost the alternative should be within their means.

The transition from a traditional to a modern economy is bound to be difficult. It would inevitably involve a certain amount of dislocation and uprooting; each major alteration will be accompanied by tensions, fears, and anxieties. In the transitional phase, which would mark the weakening of traditional norms without having at the same time an alternative set of modern norms fully developed, the socialization, consensus, and surveillance mechanisms of the society will be considerably impaired. There will perhaps be a brief stage during which the society will appear to drift. Freed from traditional controls and sanctions, and without having grasped fully the new ones, youth may show symptoms of aimlessness. Up to a degree this is unavoidable. And so, perhaps, is a certain amount of disintegration of larger kin-groups and a certain degree of decline in the observance of ritual. Norms governing behaviour linked to age, sex, and status are also certain to undergo deep changes. This would cause dislocation and resentment. Industrialization and urbanization, in their early unregulated phase, are likely to generate ugly problems of vagrancy, delinquency, deviance, and vice. These are only some of the many social problems that can be anticipated.

They need not frighten us and freeze us into inactivity, although it would be dangerous not to be cognizant of them. Time is a great healer, and man learns to adapt himself to a new milieu. But it would be a great pity if man were to lose some of his mental and moral achievements in the process.

Economic development needs careful direction. By purposefully regulating its speed and by varying its strategy in the light of observed trends and consequences, many of its lethal effects can be avoided. Thoughtful social planning alongside of economic planning is therefore necessary. We need to have a clear image of the future, an accurate anticipation of possible trends, and a systematic watch over emergent processes. Judicious investments in the socialization process—particularly education and communications—can prepare society for the new order. This would at least reduce the intensity of the shocks that are inherent in the transition of the society to the successively higher stages of economic and technological advancement. Other aspects of social planning should be designed to take care of problems as they arise.

The inevitability of economic development cannot now be questioned, nor can its desirability be doubted. At the same time its human problems and consequences also cannot be ignored. It would be fatal to leave the future of mankind to mechanical economic determinism. The analytical powers of social science can not only predict the consequences, but can also suggest correctives. Commitment to orderly and regulated change is, therefore, urgently indicated. For this the social sciences will perhaps have to give up some of their detachment and neutrality and join the battle for a richer life for man through economic progress. To the social conscience of the thinking man also this is a great challenge. He has to approach the problem with scientific understanding, patient determination, and cool courage.

THREE

Formulating the Goals of Change

The developing nations of the world are faced today with a critical choice. Standing in the twilight of tradition and modernity, they appear to be uncertain and hesitant about their goals of change. Nostalgia for the past pulls them powerfully towards the revival and vitalization of the traditional ways of life; at the same time, the economic payoff and the material advantages of technological modernization are too tempting for them to put aside easily. They think and talk in terms of integrating and synthesizing the elements of tradition and modernity. On the surface this effort to modernize according to the distinctive genius of the people is laudable, but experience with planned change, involving heavy doses of industrialization, soon brings home to them the disquieting—and disillusioning—realization that the latent subtleties and complexities of the problem cannot be handled effectively by loose and facile thinking. At some point the ultimate choice has to be made, for an effort to have the best of both worlds can result in aimlessness and drift and can jeopardize the movement towards desired economic goals. All traditional systems can absorb a degree of modernization without visible injury, but the point is soon reached where a traditional ethos and the social requisites of far-reaching economic development and technological change become irreconcilable.

India provides an excellent case in point, although it is by no means the only country presenting these symptoms. The Indian situation, in varying degrees, is reflected in most other developing countries.

The texture of earlier Indian nationalism represented an intricate weave of calls to return to ancient glories and of promises of rapid technological advancement. On the agitational platform it was not difficult to blend these two paradoxical aims. In fact, there was little realization that there could be any disharmony between the two. But in the constructive phase of Indian nationalism the contradictions between the two are beginning to manifest themselves. Can a superstructure of modernization be built on a foundation that retains all the essentials of the traditional order? There is little evidence of systematic and analytical thinking on the subject; the general tendency is to stall and to put off answering. Given to thinking in cliches and stereotypes, the average politician can perhaps be forgiven this lapse, but the failure on the part of the planner, the social scientist, and the educationist to face the issue squarely is indeed baffling.

Take, for example, the four basic attributes of Hindu society: hierarchy based on ascription; sacred rather than secular emphases in life; a diffused rather than specific system of expectations and rewards; and the communal rather than associational character of the general social organization.

Viewing them against the declared aims of the promotion of democracy, of socialism, and of a temper of science, one is tempted to ask the question—can the traditional order, characterized by the attributes listed above, be maintained while the country pursues the objectives it has set before itself? The contradictions between the two are obvious. An ascriptive order and democracy—with diametrically opposite images of the individual—cannot go together. A temper of science would necessitate relative freedom from the inhibitions implicit in the sacred emphases of the Hindu way of life. The shift from a traditional to a modern economy would require a much sharper definition of roles and thus a greater degree of specificity in the system of expectations and rewards. Finally, a cooperative commonwealth based on ideals of democratic socialism presupposes a level of interest articulation that cannot be offered by a communal type of social organization. Fundamental changes in the traditional order are, thus, clearly indicated. Unless the country takes a series of determined steps in this direction, its economic growth and technological transformation are likely to be inhibited and considerably stunted.

This does not imply, however, that to build the new edifice it is necessary to demolish entirely the old order. The past has a way of sneaking into the present and of seeping into the future. Revolutions followed by the most ruthless of dictatorships have failed to destroy a country's roots in history. And it may be stated blandly that, within a specified time range, human lives cannot be manipulated beyond a point. The existing social base cannot be ignored: some elements from it can be used for the furtherance of the plans of progress, and some others can be vitalized towards this end. This leaves only some elements that constitute a threat to progress and, as such, need to be weeded out through a carefully drawn strategy. Two fairly obvious generalizations can be made: (*i*) no society can make an entirely new beginning—it must proceed on at least a part of the existing base and draw heavily from those parts of its cultural inventory that are conducive to economic growth and technological change; (*ii*) no traditional system can survive the process of technological modernization and economic development without some dent or injury—in almost all cases it will have to undergo a thorough transformation if it seeks rapid economic growth.

The new nations are thus left with one of the following choices: (*i*) conscious rejection of modernization, with a view to preserving and vitalizing the traditional ways of life; (*ii*) conscious rejection of the traditional order, with a view to adopting an alien model of modernization; (*iii*) deliberate regulation of the content, direction, and speed of modernizations, with a view to preserving certain specified elements of the traditional order; (*iv*) deliberate regulation of the elements of the traditional order, with a view to attaining certain specified goals of modernization.

Examples of each type of choice are known and have been documented. Several instances of tribal societies consciously rejecting Western elements in a bid to return to the pristine purity of their mythological past have been recorded. The rise of Cargo Cults and other comparable movements among them has been reported and systematically analyzed. Some developing autocracies, on the other hand, have retained only a few diacritical marks from their tradition and have decreed wholesale rejection of the past to build a new future. The last two of the four choices listed above present many uncertainties. The final choice is fraught with tensions and anxieties. Ultimately the question is one of cost-benefit ratio analysis—both in the long and in the short run. Most nations which have to choose from these alternatives are in search of an identity. They can neither disown the past nor forgo the advantages of technological modernization. The decisions to be taken are difficult: *What elements of the traditional order must they preserve, whatever the cost in terms of possible retardation of economic growth? And what measures of economic and technological modernization must they achieve, whatever the injury it may cause to the traditional order?* In the era of planned change and of deliberate stimulation of rapid progress, an unambiguous decision cannot be deferred.

SOCIAL REQUIREMENTS OF ECONOMIC DEVELOPMENT

Culture is an adaptive mechanism. It reacts to every change in the natural and social environment. This results in certain inevitable changes in the social and the cultural milieu. Even in prehistoric times, when geographical distances and physical barriers were greater, some innovations achieved a near-global diffusion. For example, with the exception of a few small and isolated pockets, the entire human world felt the impact of the Neolithic Revolution, which brought about a profound technological transformation. The diffusion of metal technologies, similarly, was considerably wide. For a variety of reasons, however, the Industrial Revolution remained confined to limited areas. The rest of the world received its benefits indirectly and that too partially, some parts receiving more than others. The new nations of the contemporary world, at varying stages of industrial development, are now anxious to catch up with the industrially more developed nations so as to be able to derive, as fully as they can, the material advantages—and through them the cultural benefits—of modern science and technology.

A utopia is easy to visualize but difficult to realize. Legislative fiats alone cannot bring about a technological revolution: social change cannot be enacted. In other words, revolutionary intentions or lofty elite formulations of the aims of change, however laudable in conception and motivation, will not by themselves generate economic development. A sound strategy of planned change must be based on recognition of social complexities, on anticipation of cultural barriers, and on a variable approach to the mechanics of implementation.

The economic infrastructures of modernization have been carefully identified. The position in respect of the social infrastructures, unfortunately, is not the same. The bearings of social structure on the rate and direction of economic development are at least vaguely recognized, but the economic gains of inputs in social overheads have not been worked out meticulously. Nevertheless, there are growing signs of the realization that the degree of social change has a significant correlation with the rate of economic development.

What, then, are the social requisites—or prerequisites—of economic development? An extremely tentative and brief formulation is attempted here.

First, a developing nation needs an identity, an image of

the future, and a sense of commitment.

Second, it should have a clear perception of the desirability of change and faith in the possibility of change. The rate of economic growth is quicker in societies where there is an expectancy of change and a sense of urgency regarding it.

Third, social flexibility is an essential precondition of economic development. Economic development involves the emergence of a wide variety of new roles and, in the absence of social flexibility—and of social mobility—recruitment to these roles is greatly hampered. In other words, these countries must consciously endeavour to achieve freedom from age-old inhibitions that go against secular and rational ends-means calculations. Obscurantism and modernization—even in limited spheres, cannot go together.

Fourth, for rapid economic growth these countries will need much more social discipline and also a series of sanctions to enforce this discipline. The road to economic development, especially at the critical "take-off" stage, is hard and requires considerable sacrifice and even some privations. An emotional preparedness to undergo these self-imposed sufferings is, therefore, necessary. And a system of rewards—not necessarily economic—and sanctions must be devised to hold the waverer, the recalcitrant, and the deviant in check.

Fifth, there should be preparedness to make considerable inputs in three major social overheads—communication, education, and health. Investments in these overheads in most developing countries have been niggardly. This is so perhaps because such investments do not produce quick results: their immediate advantages are not sufficiently tangible. It is true that the benefits of costs in these spheres have not been carefully calculated, but the basic correlations between such investments and their benefits are beginning to emerge. Wilbur Schramm, an articulate student of the application of communication to national development, has brilliantly argued the case for larger inputs in communications in his book *Mass Media and National Development* (Stanford, Stanford University Press, and Paris, UNESCO, 1964). The case for investment in education and in health can be argued with equal vigour.

Sixth, the success of plans for progress requires a dynamic and purposeful leadership. The modernizing elite in these countries must, therefore, be strengthened, and larger recruitment to its ranks ensured. Special attention will have to be given to political and bureaucratic elites as they are directly involved in crucial decisions of planning and implementation; other elite groups should not be ignored, of course.

Seventh, institution building is a key step in the process of economic development. The existing organizational framework of developing societies is hardly equipped to take on the additional responsibilities implied in long-term plans of economic development. The requirements of interest articulation and interest aggregation make the building of such institutions almost obligatory. It may be added that institution building will have to cover what Lasswell calls the surveillance, the consensus, and the socialization mechanisms of these societies.

Finally, an endeavour will have to be made to inculcate a set of attitudes and values that are conducive to economic development and modernization. Several of these have been identified. The more important among them are empathy, strong secular aspirations, achievement motivation, mobile personality, ability to compute strategies on a broad stage, interest—rather than kin—orientation, and willingness to save, invest, and take calculated risks. In sum, the ideological-motivational-institutional-organizational framework of developing societies will have to undergo a thorough overhaul if they are to take any rapid strides in the direction of modernization.

THE PROCESS OF GOAL SETTING

Ideology and hope are not the only, or even the main, determinants of the goals of a society. The experience of attempts to translate an ideology into a living social reality often acts as a great transformer and reshapes the ideology itself.

A democratic modernizer would start, therefore, with a reasonably clear conception of the ultimate goals of change, but at the same time he would keep an open mind for possible shifts in their foci through the processes of democracy. His approach will be idealistic but not doctrinaire, and in devising his strategy he will be governed by pragmatic considerations. In determining the ends and means of action, he will be sensitive to popular reaction and will, and at the same time, take account of the computations and projections of the scientists. During the incipient stage, he would concentrate more on the proximate goals, the realization of which alone can create conditions favourable for the achievement of the ultimate objectives. And he will perhaps not proceed to seek the ideal all at once; the *feasible* would get the better part of his attention. His initial investments would aim at satisfying pressing "felt needs", and at building the infrastructures of development. He would introduce changes in the "soft" or vulnerable areas that are already predisposed to change or are at least relatively less change resistant. At a later stage he would possibly introduce a few critical changes calculated to ramify and to create conditions for the acceptance of more innovations. Building up the society's capacity to absorb more science and technology would be his principal aim. While doing so he would keep an eye on the social and moral consequences of change, and would not hesitate to apply necessary correctives where indicated. And, at all stages, he would boldly make investments in attitude change.

All this cannot be done without institutional change. Imaginative institutional innovations can generate structures that will neutralise change resistant elements of the traditional framework. The process of modernization itself creates conditions that compel such change.

In the context of planned change, "goals" are not to be viewed as preordained destinations. Goal setting is a process—pragmatic, dynamic, and variable.

THE INDIAN CASE

Like most other developing countries, contemporary India is characterized by blurred images and goals. The small modernizing elite continues to have a dominant voice, but the forces of tradition and conservatism are by no means dead or even insignificant. When plans for progress fail, the appeals of obscurantism become attractive. But whatever the lip service rendered to traditional ideals and forms, the goal of modernization appears to have been generally accepted. There is, however, no consensus on the elements of tradition to be preserved and no assessment of the social costs of economic development and technological change. Thinking on these themes continues to be hazy and wishful. It would be desirable not to approach the "take-off" stage with a divided mind on these seminal issues.

The major failures have been on the education and communication fronts. Efforts in these fields lack direction; they are weak, poorly organized, and not quite in harmony with the national effort on the agricultural and industrial fronts. Their major failures are: (*i*) they have not effectively projected a positive image of the New India—of what the country wants to be, and of what it should be; (*ii*) they have not seriously tried to promote the attitudes and values that are conducive to modernization; (*iii*) a new system of rewards and sanctions, necessary for economic development and social change, has not received imaginative and careful handling on their part. In short, the emergent *surveillance*, *consensus*, and *socialization* mechanisms have not been supported and sustained by our systems of education and communications.

Nation building cannot be done by exhortation alone. Investment in purposive, imaginative, and dynamic systems of education and communications—the two are complementary—is possibly the most vital investment for future progress. For they alone can contribute to image building and image maintenance, capability building and capability maintenance, and the sanction building and sanction maintenance that a developing nation requires most. The role of education and communication is essentially supportive. They are no substitute for institutional change and meaningful developmental planning; they help only in articulation and diffusion of goals that are set by other agencies of decision making. The nonutilization of education and the various communication channels creates a gap that can frustrate the efforts of the nation builder.

FOUR

The Crisis of Leadership

In the political processes of any society its leadership has several vital roles. It plays a crucial part in the dynamics of decision making. It influences the setting of group goals and national objectives, and initiates action for their realization. It also sustains group and national interest in the targets to be achieved and helps solve foreseen and unforeseen problems in the path of their accomplishment. In the final analysis, its success is judged by its capacity to carry a sizable group with it towards full or at least partial realization of pre-set objectives.

In mature politics, where the political idiom is crystallized and the political game is played according to well-established and generally observed rules, the elbow room for manoeuvre and manipulation by the leadership is relatively limited. However, the situation in developing societies, where the social infrastructure is not geared to the largely superimposed political structure, presents a picture of fluidity which stands out in sharp contrast to that of the more mature systems. In the relative absence of interest articulation and interest aggregation, and within the framework of a still poorly developed system of political communication, the leadership acquires a more critical significance. In the quicksand of politics, emphases and strategies change with amazing rapidity. The situation presents a baffling set of dilemmas and paradoxes, and the masses look to the leadership for their solution. The leadership has very considerable manoeuvrability, and it can change its postures with little or practically no questioning from its following. In many situations the leadership is not even sensitive and responsive to the people. In some countries, it is vulnerable to public opinion, but the days of judgment with their unpredictable shocks and surprises come after five to seven-year intervals. Some leaders hope to ensure their survival by holding out new promises in the shape of appealing slogans and attractive programmes. Past utopias and recipes for progress are conveniently forgotten, and new ones are offered with reckless abandon.

Indian democracy, although it has proved itself more stable and successful than many new democracies in Asia and Africa, is undergoing an acute crisis of leadership. The first two elections in free India were held during the phase of reverent affirmation. In the euphoria of independence, the people had the vision of a glorious future, without any consciousness of the constraints and responsibilities of freedom. Voting was an act of homage to Gandhi, to Nehru, and to the host of freedom fighters who had led the country to national independence. They had fulfilled the promise of freedom and they could be looked upon also to fulfil the promise of prosperity. The image of the leader continued to be predominantly that of the self-sacrificing patriot who was a cut above the common man.

By the time of the third general elections there was a visible change ir the mood of the masses. Their gods had disappointed if not failed, them. The performance of the leadership was significantly inadequate on many fronts. Many in their ranks were seen as what they really were—seekers after power trying to entrench themselves in positions of authority, irrespective of their ability to solve problems. Charisma, even that of some of the well-established leaders, was vanishing; one by one, they were coming down from their high pedestals. This was the phase of critical compliance. Frustrations were mounting, but the point of explosion had not been reached. Nehru's charisma—although not wholly untarnished—had survived. Because of him, and also perhaps because people had not seriously looked for an alternative, the party in power was granted an extension in office, although not without reservations.

The temper of the electorate had undergone a violent change at the time of the third general election. Discontent had developed into anger, and the electorate was ready to register a major protest. The ballot was an instrument of this protest. An alternative was not yet within sight; nevertheless, to many, a massive protest was in order. The results were unnerving even to those who had, in the past, not ordinarily lost their equanimity and self-confidence. The tenuous course of Indian democracy after this election is too recent to need any recounting. The politics of relentless pressure and mob violence has raised serious misgivings about the suitability of the parliamentary apparatus of democracy to contemporary Indian conditions.

What has been the overall performance of the leadership in India? It has placed before the people a set of national goals and objectives but, because of ineffective channels of communication—and organizational inadequacies—they have not reached down to the common people. In any case, a sense of commitment to these objectives has not been generated. The action of the leadership has often lacked determination and, in consequence, efforts to implement policies and plans have been shaky and their results feeble. Perhaps its greatest failure has been its inability to arouse and sustain interest even in respect of major objectives. Its incapacity to foresee problems was remarkable, and its efforts to handle them were characterized by naivete and indecision. In sum, as an agency of decision making and decision enforcement it fumbled time and again, creating in the minds of people the image of a spineless body that was a prisoner of its own indecision. In retrospect, an attempt may be made to analyze some of the causes of these failures.

The pre-independence leadership was geared more to creating solidarity than to problem solving. Agitation was the dominant note of its strategy. Although from among its ranks some individuals emerged with a remarkable capacity for statesmanship, the bulk did not attune itself to the demands of the complex problems that awaited solution. Many who had outlived their utility were allowed to continue in positions of responsibility. This dead wood of Indian politics used its position of vantage to impart to itself a degree of indispensability. Leadership continued to be functionally diffuse: the climate was unfavourable to the growth of functionally specific leadership. As a near abject surrender was expected from those potentially able to provide leadership in problem solving fields by those in political authority, a complementary leadership could not develop. Thus, the reserves of creative thinking in the country were never exploited. The leaders of earlier agitations took over many complex responsibilities for which they were not suited in terms of their experience, knowledge, and skill. A section of the leadership, which did not have access to political power, continued to follow agitational methods without any constructive problem solving aids.

India's search for a new identity was disturbed by the inner contradictions in the leadership. Many among those who occupied leadership positions at different levels were all too ready to pay lip service to the ideals preached by the country's two towering leaders, only one of whom lived long enough to mastermind the country's future. Few dissenting voices were raised, but the formal acceptance of Nehru's ideology and programme did not in any sense imply a serious or genuine commitment to them. The facade of a revolutionary world-view hid a bewildering series of parochial pulls and trends. A few ill-timed concessions contributed immeasurably to the strengthening of parochial tendencies. In the name of pragmatism, narrow and sectarian loyalties were exploited to the detriment of national integration. Casteism, linguism, regionalism, communalism, and tribalism, among others, were the fruit of myopic strategies that were pursued when the country was ostensibly committed to the very opposite ideals. The injury to the goals of socialism and secularism was, perhaps, more serious. To many they were convenient slogans but inconvenient operational philosophies. Massive social action was never engineered to invest a sense of reality into the ideals that were preached. In consequence, today the country lacks a sense of direction. It is significant that many parochial sentiments stealthily exploited by the dominant party are now being openly promoted by some opposition parties.

Over the years the fabric of leadership has undergone a qualitative change. Those who stood by the old ideals of sacrifice and service either voluntarily left active politics to take up humanitarian work of the "constructive" variety or were eased out of its mainstream. In their place political "bosses" emerged who could control the party machine, organize factional politics, raise funds, and engineer the elections. For many years the true power of these party bosses remained unrecognized, and even the top leaders were not aware of how far these lesser known but well-entrenched men had spread their tentacles. Their invisible power gradually began to be felt: the interests they represented started asserting themselves. The accepted ideology was never formally renounced, but its implementation showed unmistakable signs of the new pressures. Of course, the old idealistic fervour could not last indefinitely: in the emerging political scene the politician had to learn to calculate better and to bargain harder. These are features of all mature political systems. However, in the Indian case no limits were set and no rules of the game were evolved. Pious resolutions were passed from time to time, but changes in policies were also frequent. Exigencies of the given situation often dictated the decision. Thus, many could disregard formally accepted principles and rules with impunity. Recruitment to political roles—especially around the seats of power at different levels—was quick, but the political socialization of the new entrants was characterized by a cognitive dissonance that came in the way of the development of high quality leadership. Revolt against the power monopoly of one party—or a reaction to barred doors—swelled the ranks of the growing number of opposition parties, but like the dominant party most of them also lacked inner cohesion. The harassed bosses of the ruling party derived some satisfaction from the divisiveness present in almost all the opposition parties.

A disturbing feature of the emerging ethos was the new political style which was characterized by an almost total lack of restraint and discipline. The attainment of power is one of the principal ends of all political activity, but the means are always governed and conditioned by considerations of legitimacy. The quest for power ungoverned by rules of legitimacy created a situation that alarmed a section of the more thoughtful element of the society. Parochial issues were pursued with a passion that deserved better causes. Scarce resources and national property were destroyed without compunction. Serious national issues that merited rational thought by those who had special knowledge and skills were sought to be decided by mass demonstrations and mob violence. Civic life was paralyzed and production was brought to a standstill on trivial pretexts. An unfortunate impression gained ground that only these methods succeed in shaking an immobile government out of its inertia. Leaders of thought and action appeared to stand by helplessly watching the situation. Perhaps they felt that the fury would spend itself and that conditions would return to normal. At any rate, there was no convincing evidence of purposeful action to stem the tide of the forces that ran counter to all canons of democracy.

For a long time the macro-political system of India functioned as a practically autonomous system without any organic links with the micro-political systems. National politics was a largely urban phenomenon and it reached down to the grassroots only during elections. Few political parties had a strong mass base in the rural areas. For the purpose of getting votes, dyadic relations in the resource network were geared into action. Rather than create new channels most parties utilized existing ones. Appeals were routed mostly through channels of caste and factional affiliation. In some cases appeals to caste sentiments worked and caste-clusters voted together; in others, village factions and inter-village faction-chains provided the rallying force. Village leaders, who traditionally functioned as patrons, arbitrators/mediators, and brokers, extended their traditional functions to act as middlemen between macro and micro-politics. Inter-caste and inter-faction rivalries were often deftly exploited. Considerations of adding to their own or to their faction's power weighed more with the village leaders than did political convictions.

But power alignments in the villages are imperceptibly changing and new links are being forged between macro and micro-politics. Village leaders are becoming increasingly aware of their importance, and the three-tier system of panchayati raj institutions has provided them with avenues to participate in the wider political arena. The processes are complex and cannot be comprehended through simplistic explanations. For example, the notion that dominant castes control "vote banks" contains several fallacies. Apart from the fact that faction membership is in many villages more relevant than caste membership in the context of power, the so-called "dominant castes" have to make so many vital concessions to the non-dominant groups that they hardly qualify for the appellation given to them. Caste may provide a convenient rallying point; but power is sought by individuals, and considerations of factional gain are not divested from it. A new source of recruitment to political cadres is added, but actual political affiliations are dictated more by considerations of short-run power gains than by long-range political objectives. An unintended consequence of the new agricultural policy has been to strengthen some aspirants for power in the villages and enable them to assume increasingly important political roles.

India's political system, as it exists today, has an amorphous character. It has links with the traditional social structure, but the two are not enmeshed. They tend to operate in separate spheres. The political system, however, has made important concessions to the social system and has done very little to attune it to a democratic ethos. In the absence of functionally specific interest groups, personalities continue to dominate the political scene and contextual exigencies continue to dominate strategies. In this personalized order, ideological commitment and articulation are weak, and there is little evidence of their getting stronger. The tasks of reconciliation are becoming increasingly complex and difficult, and the mobilizing functions being performed in the political system are more for short-run, narrow, and parochial objectives than for the broader objectives that are of vital concern to the nation's future. The symptoms of a national malaise are recognized, but no determined therapeutical action appears to be taken about them.

FIVE

Role of the Intelligentsia in Newly Independent Countries

When European powers, spurred first by their growing naval capability and later by the need to find markets for the products of the Industrial Revolution, started carving out their spheres of influence in lands across the seas and laying down foundations for later colonial conquests, their targets were internally divided and were unable to cope with the challenges of a changing world. They were specially vulnerable on the economic frontier; this facilitated relatively easy penetration of the Europeans through trade and commerce. The tradition of religious toleration in many of these countries permitted entry to proselytizers motivated by the urge to reclaim the souls of native pagans.

Trade and religion invariably got enmeshed in power

intrigues; internal dissensions had created a climate propitious for the success of their combined operations. The emerging colonial powers slowly strengthened their hold and consolidated their position by a series of interventions—some by invitation, others on account of some real or assumed provocations, and still others only for gaining political and administrative control. To stabilize and sustain their political control, with a view to deriving direct and indirect benefits from it, the imperial powers had to initiate varied and often devious policies.

The countries that became colonies in one form or other had a weak social fibre. Invariably their social structure was stratified and segmented. Ascription was the principal criterion of stratification, although it did not always flow from the ritual idiom. Power and wealth were important determinants of status, and elite and non-elite differences were significant.

The elites, in the early phase of colonialism, consisted of the *dynastic elite*, including major satellites and chains of minor satellites; the *ritual elite*, with a monopoly over sacred learning and priestly functions; the *business elite*, mostly with a trader ethic; and the *rural elite*, consisting of minor satellites of the dynastic elite at the rural fringe, and of the landed gentry.

The process of consolidation of imperialism influenced the elite structure in two ways: first, it reinforced the traditional elites; and second, it created avenues for the emergence of new elites.

Continued recognition of the power and the privileges (somewhat curtailed and put under imperial surveillance) of the dynastic elite, symbolic recognition of status by graded gun salutes, treaty relations binding them into allegiance, conferment of honorific titles, and so forth, were aimed at causing minimal dislocation in the traditional position of the dynastic elite while aligning it firmly with the imperial power. The major and minor satellites also received certain benefits: secure land rights, restricted administrative powers, and grant of lesser titles. Loyalty was a precondition of the continuance of these benefits. The business elite found a stable administrative and judicial system to its advantage; those sections of it which showed special concern for the imperial power and its agents were also invested with some marks of social distinction. This was the position also in the case of the landed gentry in rural areas. The ritual elite did not receive much direct benefit but had reason to be grateful, because there was no frontal attack on its position and privileges.

The growing needs of the colonial system and, possibly, its humanitarian impulses and notions of justice, necessitated the creation of opportunities for the emergence of new elites. These elites consisted of: (*i*) the *administrative elite*, the upper and middle rungs of colonial administration, drawn from those natives who had received a Western style of education; (*ii*) the *professional elite*, especially in the legal and medical professions, which was trained in the newly established educational institutions; (*iii*) the *intellectual elite*, which on the one hand had a new awareness of the country's cultural heritage, and on the other was exposed to the powerful currents of ideas shaping the modern world; and (*iv*) the *political elite*, comprising two major streams—nationalist leaders, subsuming their divergent ideologies and objectives under the overriding goal of national independence, and the revolutionary intellectuals, who were not fully reconciled either to the goals of the nationalists or to the means adopted by them.

The emergence of these new elites should not be viewed as a disjunctive process. It provided avenues to the traditional elites to enter high-prestige vocations. The dynastic elites as well as the propertied and ritually privileged groups were better situated to take advantage of the new opportunities. The lesser dynastic elites and the two other elite groups did so, in fact, on a large scale. The ranks of the new elites did not represent an extension of a pre-existing closed system: the walls were still there, but now they had small apertures for others also to enter and to gain status on the achievemental plane. The recruitment base was still largely associated with the traditional elites, but the primacy of the performance criterion was a commendable feature of the process of elevation to the new elite ranks. Another conjunctive trend was represented by the emergence of some entrepreneurs among the business elite and their shift from trade to industry.

New developments in the social system inspired and supported by the colonial powers were not without internal stresses and strains. Some segments, mostly the products of institutions promoted by the system, began questioning the legitimacy and the desirability of the colonial order. An anti-colonial movement was born. During the initial phase it lacked solidarity and articulation, but it certainly created a mood for the expression of dissent. A loyal/non-loyal dichotomy was created; the latter continued to gather momentum and strength.

The new elites constituted the intelligentsia—a category consisting of the educated portion of the population and regarded as being capable of shaping public opinion. This category was subsumed largely in the elusive "middle class", although it had identifiable strata based on income and influence.

Four segments of the intelligentsia were important and, in time, each of them came to be identified with certain functions. The functions of these segments, during this phase, were the following :

Segment	*Functions*
Bureaucracy	(*i*) Maintenance of order
	(*ii*) Management; operationalizing goals and strategies
	(*iii*) Attainment of limited nation building and welfare objectives
Political Leadership	(*i*) Goal setting
	(*ii*) Mobilization
	(*iii*) Solidarity building
	(*iv*) Strategy control
Intellectuals	(*i*) Transmission of knowledge and development of problem solving abilities
	(*ii*) Interpretation
	(*iii*) Production of new knowledge
	(*iv*) Social criticism
The Professions	(*i*) Sectoral modernization
	(*ii*) Adaptation and innovation

Alongside the administrative bureaucracy—the civil service—a class of *managers* who worked for the growing industries was also emerging. Its functions were developing along independent lines—guidance in entrepreneurship, management (including adaptation and innovation), enlargement of the profit base and capital formation, and sectoral modernization.

Each of these segments created an ethos of its own and, by working out patterns of interaction with the traditional elite, tried to develop for itself a role in the emerging social structure.

Bureaucracy, although it was not the fountainhead of power, continued to grow because in its instrumental role it had considerable initiative and manipulative scope within a given broad policy framework. Over the years it enlarged its power and perquisites. In general its tone was authoritarian, and it tended to maintain a distance between itself as a category and the people at large whom it ruled. Its style of life was moulded into a pattern different from that of the common people. Many of the changes were superficial and imitative, more in the nature of diacritical marks than as indicators of fundamental transformations in cultural emphases. It did tend, however, to emerge as a marginal group, more prone than most towards a rational and secular outlook.

The political leadership was a mixed group. Ideologically diverse and apparently irreconcilable groups had joined together for the attainment of a limited objective—national liberation. The obscurantist and the rationalist, the mystic and the revolutionary, the pragmatist and the utopian, all of these could gather under the umbrella of nationalism. The miracle was that this strange amalgam worked and produced results. But it had its dysfunctional aspects too. The veneer of nationalism, in the case of some, could barely hide their communalism. The revivalists glorified the past to such an extent that a balanced appraisal of the contemporary predicament became impossible. Schisms within the movement generated contrary pressures. Thinking in regard to the economic, political, and cultural character of the nation to be built tended to be hazy. The accent was on solidarity building, not on problem solving. Another political leadership, opposed to the nationalists and serving imperial interests at least indirectly, was also being encouraged—if not sponsored—by the foreign rulers.

The intellectuals, as a category, hardly had a personality. Knowledge was being diffused, but there was little attempt to assess either its content or its consequences. In many fields it combined the parochial and the universal. The interpretation function expressed itself in appeals for revivalism or for reform, often both at the same time. There were some notable attempts towards a synthesis of traditional culture and the rationalism and science of the West, but in all such efforts one or other of the two elements asserted itself and became dominant. There was not much independent social criticism, but within the framework either of imperialism or of nationalism, a dialogue on some important social and economic issues was initiated. This invariably carried the imprint of the side to which the contributor was aligned. Production of new knowledge in science was confined to a small number of centres. There was considerable development in historical, philosophical, and other humanistic studies, all motivated by the quest for a national identity. Survey and exploration added to the fund of knowledge, but interpretation remained weak. There was either too much self-conscious imitation of the style of scholarship in the ruling country or a great deal of frothy and short-sighted nationalism.

The professions contributed towards limited modernization in their respective spheres. They also provided recruits to the ranks of political leadership. It is significant that those from the legal and medical professions occupied high places in the political elite of many developing countries.

It is to be remembered, however, that the colonial policies in different countries were based on different approaches and followed different principles. This accounted for some significant differences in the evolution of the intelligentsia, in elite/non-elite ratios, and in the articulation of their goals.

INDEPENDENCE AND AFTER

For a time the euphoria of independence kept the discrete elements together, but the emerging power equations were reshaping elite alignments and their operating cultures. In perspective, one can now visualize considerable interpenetration of elites, role reversals, redefinition of goals, and modification of styles. The size of the intelligentsia increased manifold and this had important consequences.

The dynastic elites, with their extensive networks, first took only tentative steps towards the political arena, but later joined forces and jumped into it. In some countries, of course, they had readymade roles, but even in democratic countries they tried to carve for themselves a major political role. In their respective pockets of influence, they registered impressive success. The rural elite, especially the landed gentry, emerged as a considerable political force; it had a decisive voice in shaping policies, or at least in diluting and delaying the implementation of policies that carried a threat for them. The ritual elite also imparted a distinct flavour to politics; the assumption of a secular role by traditionally sacred categories often produced some bizarre results. At any rate, their potential for mischief was considerable. The participation of the business and the industrial elites was both direct and indirect. Some magnates and their agents entered and won elections, but the indirect influence they exercised—by extending financial backing to individual candidates and parties through their lobbies and through their control over the mass media—was substantial. There is evidence also of the political elite acquiring a dynastic character in some countries. Its style of life was changing; Soekarno and Nkrumah, for example, lived in regal splendour that would put to shame some major potentates. Even in countries whose political traditions emphasized self-denial and simplicity, these styles were cultivated under various pretexts. Some from their ranks entered commerce and industry and registered an astonishingly rapid rise.

As if to confuse the already complicated situation, a new form of imperialism was asserting itself. It had a bagful of tricks, ranging from subtle blandishments to blatant threats. Economic aid was its principal instrument, but it never came without invisible or visible strings. It influenced the content and the course of state policy significantly. This was not all; the attack, in fact, was many-pronged. There was a battle for minds, aimed at perpetuating academic colonialism. Business and industry were offered partnership for profit. Under different garbs administration and management were influenced. Predisposed and interested political leaders and parties were sustained. In the long run, the newly independent countries could not develop a genuine spirit of self-reliance. They were being reduced to clients or satellite status.

What was happening to the intelligentsia? How was it redefining its role? In the new context, how was it contributing to the consolidation of independence and to economic development?

Bureaucracy found itself encapsulated in the new political culture, but it continued to live in a make-believe world of its own. The political environment was changing rapidly. The higher civil servant, however, found himself unable to move with the times. He was not able to cope adequately even with the problems of order, a field considered his speciality. His methods worked admirably in a *subject* political culture; in a *participant* political culture they created as many problems as they solved. But the shift of emphasis, from order to welfare and development, exposed its weaknesses further. In the new functions—of goal setting and goal definition, of entrepreneurship and management, and of evaluation and adaptation—bureaucracy demonstrated what Veblen would call "trained incapacity". The more important factors accounting for its inadequacy and failure were insulation from the people, excessive concern for power and privilege, commitment to rules and procedure rather than to results, misplaced faith in the capabilities of the generalist administrator, and inability to adapt to the emerging idiom. In its handling of policy framed by the political elite there were significant goal displacements and goal transfers. In certain fields it has served well, but its dysfunctional aspects cannot be ignored.

The record of the political leadership is also not without blemishes. In the early years of freedom, when mass political participation was little more than homage to heroes of the liberation struggle, the leadership acquired a taste for power and for high living; it lost, in the process, much of its earlier idealism, service motivation, and spirit of sacrifice. Later, when the voter became more critical, it took recourse to subterfuge. It had handled the freedom movement effectively, but in applying its functions to nation building it faltered.

Its principal weaknesses were excessive self-orientation, gaps between profession and practice, unscrupulousness in exploiting parochial issues for short term political gains, inability to effect major structural changes, and insensitivity to mass urges. In many newly independent countries, military regimes took over. Although initially they adopted radical postures, it did not take them too long to reveal their true identities. In a few countries, governments more responsive to popular urges and capable of taking hard decisions are emerging. Their performance remains to be judged.

The intellectuals have continued to transmit knowledge; much of it is, however, obsolete and not relevant to the problems of their country. Their contribution to interpretation has often been puerile, lacking both perception and depth. The new knowledge that has been produced has wavered between the trite and the trivial. Even the better scholars have cultivated "international" styles that adorn the pages of learned journals rather than serve the pressing needs of the country. And there has been little meaningful social criticism. In the scholarly effort one misses a sense of urgency, mission, and participation. The professions too have shown no eagerness to serve, nor have they evinced partisan interest in national development.

This picture is gloomy indeed, but so also is the prevailing situation. In how many countries has the intelligentsia given a good account of itself? How many newly independent countries have been able to consolidate their freedom in the quarter century following the attainment of national independence?

The major task before newly independent countries can be summed up as "growth with justice". This would involve developing a spirit of self-reliance and fighting all influences—visible and invisible—that have a corroding influence on the emergence of such a spirit. Nation building requires, on the one hand, holding in check all divisive forces; on the other, it needs the development of problem solving capabilities. In both, the role of the intelligentsia is clear. It comprises: (*i*) *goal setting and goal definition*—precise formulation of the proximate and ultimate objectives of national policy; (*ii*) *communication and mobilization*—informing and arousing the masses for participation; (*iii*) *organization and management*—developing resources and capabilities, adaptation and production of knowledge, and ensuring their optimum utilization; (*iv*) *tension management*—minimizing injuries of change and handling stress-producing situations; (*v*) *fighting subversion of freedom*—especially from outside, coming in several disguises; and (*vi*) *evaluation and growth*—keeping a watch on the intended and unintended consequences of policies, and tilting the latter towards progressive goals.

The questions before newly independent countries are those of survival with dignity and of growth without subservience. All need major structural change and a purposive leadership that can take and enforce hard decisions. Towards the attainment of these objectives the intelligentsia can make a meaningful contribution. This it can do if it gives itself a purposive reorientation and takes up its role with commitment. A democratic policy would not insist on rigid uniformity, but a broad consensus on key issues is a must.

SIX

Bureaucracy and Nation Building

Bureaucracy forms an important element of the modernizing elite in many of the economically less developed countries which have attained national independence during the last two decades. Trained in the colonial tradition, this organized and articulate segment of the native society functioned as a bridge between the dependent indigenous people and the ruling power from the West. Although it had to work under the direction of the imperial power and had largely to carry out its policies, it was not without nationalist sentiments and aspirations. Held suspect during the days of the struggle for freedom both by politically oriented countrymen and by the alien rulers, members of this class had, by and large, acquired a progressive orientation. The more sophisticated among them had definite ideas regarding the programmes of economic and social development to be adopted by their country on the attainment of national independence. In many countries they were the only organized body of natives with considerable training and experience in administration; they naturally found themselves called upon to assume major responsibilities in the formulation and implementation of national plans for economic development and social change.

The general change in the political climate, the assumption of power by the political elite, the changing alignments of power and pressure groups, and the emergence of new institutional and administrative patterns raised in their wake a series of complex problems for bureaucracy. In consequence, it had to make some significant adjustments in its ways of thought and its work and to adapt itself to the new ethos. On the other hand, in many sensitive areas it found itself either openly resisting some of the new elements or accepting them only theoretically. Thus, with or without the overt acceptance of the new patterns, it stood for the continuity of some of the established norms. In meeting these intricate problems of adjustment and value-conflict, the character of bureaucracy in transitional societies is undergoing a rapid change. Since it occupies a pivotal position in these societies, and will continue to do so in the foreseeable future, an understanding of the character and culture of bureaucracy is essential for those concerned with the programmes of economic growth and social change in the economically less developed countries.

Planning for economic growth is an extremely complicated business which involves highly specialized knowledge and developed manipulative skills; the implementation of these plans presupposes deep administrative insights and a keen evaluative perspective. In the context of the programmes of community development, it is common these days to emphasize the ideal of planning by the people, but the crucial fact that this stage must necessarily be preceded by the stages of planning *for* the people and planning *with* the people is not given sufficient emphasis. The acceptance of these three stages means successively diminishing functions for the bureaucracy in matters of local and regional planning and in developmental administration, but it is essential to bear in mind that the gap between the first and the third stages is very considerable and that the transition to the final stage depends largely upon the manner in which the process is initiated and the first two stages carried out. Both these stages involve considerable direct participation by bureaucracy; the second stage particularly—which requires the initiation of a process of withdrawal—has critical significance. Optimism, bordering on wishful thinking, cannot alone diminish the importance of bureaucracy; its role in the process of planning and developmental administration is bound to figure prominently for several decades. The problem of the integration of local, regional, and national plans demands knowledge and skills which perhaps only bureaucracy possesses. Of course, as the process acquires greater complexity the technocrat is drawn into it more deeply for, without the utilization of his specialized knowledge, planning for successive stages would become increasingly difficult. Nevertheless, much maligned and distrusted as it is, bureaucracy is not without a vital role to play in the process of planning for economic and social development. Modifications in its structure, values, and method of work are necessary to adapt it to the idiom of the fast changing situation, but the fact remains that it cannot be done away with. An understanding of its character and the initiation of imaginative plans for changing its structure and values so as to make it a more effective instrument for development must, therefore, be considered an essential prerequisite to planned change in these countries.

Discriminatingly recruited on the basis of specified criteria and carefully trained according to established and time-tested plans, bureaucracies in most of the former colonies and dependencies became efficient instruments of administration. Although they were oriented more to functions of law and order and the collection of revenues, they were also entrusted from time to time with some nation building responsibilities. In discharging their responsibilities they showed all the classical characteristics of bureaucracies: they were formally organized with unambiguous demarcation of roles and statuses, and were articulated to clearly defined goals; they were efficient and equipped with the required knowledge; they were well-versed in formal rules of procedure and recognized their predominance; and, finally, they were trained to function in an impersonal manner under conditions of near-anonymity.

In addition to the above, bureaucracies in these societies had certain special characteristics. In their respective countries they were perhaps the first large and organized groups to enter the transitional phase between tradition and modernity—the twilight zone lying between societal types, described variously in continue such as communal-associational, sacred-secular, status-contract, and *gemeinschaft-gesellschaft*. In other words, they were among the pioneers who sought to break away from the traditionally affective and emotion-based communal society and to set in motion the forces that were to contribute towards the emergence of a different type of society—a society characterized by affective neutrality and based on rational ends-means calculations for individual goals. As distinct subcultural entities within the larger frameworks of their societies, they were at least partly absolved from the traditional obligation of having to share communal attitudes, sentiments, and repressive authority and were among the first to constitute groups characterized by specialized division of labour, by different but complementary interests and sentiments, and by restrictive authority. It is not suggested here that they could break away completely from tradition to adopt the ideals and values of modernity; in the critical areas of choice making, they had before them a wide zone of fluid values in which were present the elements both of tradition and of modernity. The logic and rationale of selectivity in the process of choice making has not been analyzed in depth, but the fact that, gradually and in an increasing measure, bureaucracy adopted several elements of modernity is not without significance.

It might be useful to describe here some special features of these bureaucracies as they emerged and crystallized during the colonial phase.

Bureaucracy constituted a special sub-cultural segment—the high prestige stratum of the society. Entrance to it was theoretically not barred to any section of the community although, in actual practice, only the traditionally privileged could provide the necessary general background and the expensive education required for success in the stiff tests prescribed for entry into its higher echelons. In limited numbers, others also gained entrance into the relatively closed group of higher civil servants. Middle level and lower positions in it attracted the less privileged. Bureaucracy had a class bias and it tended to have a stratification of its own;

its upper crust functioned as a privileged class. On the whole it symbolized achievement rather than ascription. Over time it came to have distinct vested interests and was sensitive to all threats to its position and privileges, which it guarded jealously against encroachment from any quarter.

It existed largely in the twilight zone of cultures. Partly traditional and partly modern, it could and did choose from the elements of both. In several ways it was alienated from the masses and uprooted from the native cultural traditions; significant differences in styles of living and in modes of thought separated the two. The Western rulers, on the other hand, never conceded equality to it. In consequence, bureaucracy maintained dual identification and was characterized by a dual ambivalence.

Besides offering security of tenure and relatively higher emoluments, bureaucratic positions carried vast powers which made them additionally attractive and important. The powers vested in a minor functionary gave him prestige, perquisites, and privileges far beyond those justified by his emoluments and his position in the hierarchy. Formally the roles and statuses of functionaries at different levels were defined, but in actual practice the system of expectation and obligation between them tended to be diffused rather than specific.

Within the framework of the overall policy laid down by the imperial power, in day-to-day administration the bureaucratic machine enjoyed considerable freedom from interference. Thus, there were few hindrances to its exercise of power, which was often authoritarian in tone and content. Bureaucracy had, in general, a paternalistic attitude to the masses. The masses, on their part, accepted the position and looked to the administration for a wide variety of small favours.

Administration was concerned mainly with the collection of land revenue and the maintenance of law and order. The general administrator under these conditions enjoyed supremacy. Subject matter specialists of welfare and nation building departments were relegated to secondary positions and functioned under the guidance and control of the generalist.

Bureaucracy was carefully trained in formal administrative procedure and routine. Stereotypes in this sphere were well-developed and were scrupulously observed.

In the limited framework of its functions and its set procedures, bureaucracy formed a self-contained system. It resented and resisted innovations.

Its attitude to the nationalist forces within was most ambivalent. Few within the bureaucracy were devoid of patriotic sentiments and aspirations, but only in rare exceptions could they side openly with the forces of nationalism. The requirements of their official positions made them an instrument for the execution of imperialist policies. This naturally aroused in the nationalist leadership feelings of anger and distrust against them. This rejection, by the leaders of the nationalist forces, as well as by the politically conscious masses, was largely at the root of their ambivalent attitude towards the nationalist forces.

Bureaucracy welcomed the advent of independence as much as any other group in the former colonies and dependencies, but the first years of freedom were for it a period of great stress and strain. It had covertly resented Western domination, but in the first decade of independence it remained under the shadow of suspicion because of its former association and identification with the alien power. While its power and prestige were decreasing, its burdens and responsibilities were increasing. Attacked from several sides simultaneously and with mounting pressure, bureaucracy found itself in a difficult and uncomfortable position.

The more important areas in which it had to work for a redefinition and consequent readjustment of its position and responsibilities were the culture of politics, the emerging ethos, and the expanding sphere of State activity and the new institutional arrangements.

THE CULTURE OF POLITICS

In the new order the supremacy of administration was replaced largely by the sovereignty of politics. Politics became the most important activity and the politician came to occupy a position of unquestionable supremacy in matters of decision making. Within the framework of this culture of politics, there was an unmistakable tendency towards the merging of political roles with personal and social roles; the expectations of the politician from his followers and administrative subordinates were diffused. Politics centred round individuals; informal factions or groups formed around key personalities were more meaningful units of political organization than the formal structures of political parties. Personal loyalty to politicians, under these conditions, played an important part in the process of political identification and decision making. Administration under such leadership could not remain wholly impersonal. The political elite was nurtured more in the politics of agitation than in the politics of nation building, and as a hangover from the past it persisted in its agitational approach. Nucleated around individuals, political processes lacked organic unity; communication was not adequately articulated. In general, political parties represented some kind of a revolutionary world view and philosophy, and on larger international and national issues they stood for an unlimited utopia. On specific issues, especially of a regional or local character, the position was significantly different; political opinion on them was often narrow, sectarian, and parochial. Thus, political thinking regarding issues at different levels lacked cohesion and integration. The attitude of the political elite was characterized by ambivalence. They sought to work for modernization without giving up their love for tradition; attempts to harmonize, synthesize, and integrate the elements of the two, even on a conceptual level, were neither systematic nor serious.

In many countries the bureaucracy was trained well enough to accept political direction, and only in a few exceptional cases did it try to gain the upper hand. Adjustment and adaptation to this political culture, however, was not without its problems. The new order posed a definite threat to bureaucracy's structure, values, and interests. While its formal structure remained intact, the definition of roles and statuses within the hierarchy was disturbed by the emergence of the politician as the focal point of decision making. The personal nature of political decision making was another unsettling factor. It not only affected the internal status system of bureaucracy, but also sometimes bypassed its special knowledge and side-tracked its procedural routine. In many specific contexts administration could not function in an impersonal manner. Inter-personal relations between the politician and the administrator tended to be uneasy. The politician recognized the value and importance of bureaucracy, but he continued to have a definite antagonism towards it, to exhort and admonish it to change its ways, and to ridicule it for some of its modes of thought and action that were out of tune with the new order. Much of this criticism was valid, but the manner in which it was made was often irritating to bureaucrats. Many members of bureaucracy had silently admired the self-sacrificing patriots as heroes but, in close proximity, saw them without the halo that had surrounded them during the days of the national struggle. Often, the gap between their profession and their practice particularly annoyed the perceptive members of bureaucracy. The politician was himself adopting much of what he criticized in the bureaucrat. Some members of the administration were all too willing to adapt, but their over-readiness to do so was viewed by the discerning administrator as a dangerous departure that could undermine the character and role of bureaucracy.

THE EMERGING ETHOS

The emerging ethos also presented bureaucracy with a series of problems. In the new setting it could not maintain its image of power, nor could it continue to exist as a high prestige class enjoying exceptional privileges. A closer identification with the masses was called for; the authoritarian tone of administration had also to change. On a theoretical and emotional level the desirability of this change was conceded, but a system of rationalization was developed at the same time to justify the maintenance of the *status quo*. Today a great contradiction persists between emotional awareness of the desirable and willingness to accept it in practice.

THE EXPANDING SPHERE OF STATE ACTIVITY

The structure, values, and working methods of bureaucracy in almost all former colonies and dependencies were geared to law and order and to revenue administration, for which it was efficiently trained. Administration for nation building necessitated a different approach involving a new value orientation and a modified institutional set-up. It is in these spheres that the failures of bureaucracy are perhaps the most pronounced.

By and large bureaucracy resists innovations in its structural arrangements. It appears to have a firm faith in the superiority of the pyramidal structure of administration and in the infallibility of the generalist. Efforts to nuclearize the administration for nation building are resented, and so is any attempt to dislodge the general administrator from his high pedestal. Concepts of inner-democratization, of administrative decentralization, and of delegation of authority and responsibility receive at best only lip service. Coordination becomes difficult because of faulty communication between the general administrator and the technical specialist. Effective utilization of the specialist is blocked by the accepted or assumed supremacy of the general administrator whose self-confidence borders almost on arrogance. The latter, perhaps, realizes that he is not trained for certain jobs, but he rarely concedes this publicly. Innovations have been made in these spheres, but the marks of bureaucratic resistance are still evident.

Subconsciously, perhaps the bureaucrat still believes in the efficacy of the traditional approach to administration. New approaches are discussed and half-heartedly accepted, but only in rare cases do they receive a fair trial. Extension and community development approaches, for instance, have encountered considerable resistance from bureaucracy. Indeed, many members of the administration would be glad to revert to type, and would willingly reverse the process that has gained partial acceptance for these approaches after years of experimentation and persuasion.

It is generally recognized that the cumbrous administrative routine, good in its time, today practically immobilizes developmental administration. Yet all attempts to change the rules of procedure result invariably in the formulation of rules that are as complex as those they seek to replace, if not more so. Efforts at deconcentration of power, such as the experiment of democratic decentralization for development in India, meet with even greater resistance. Doubtless the infant "grassroots democracy" is not without shortcomings, but its threats to the perpetuation of bureaucratic vested interests have alerted the administrator, whose approach to the experiment is extremely guarded, wooden, and unimaginative.

Attempts have been made at reorienting bureaucracy to the new philosophy of administration, but they have often been viewed as mere short-lived fads and fancies. Indirectly the new approach has made some headway, but there is little evidence to suggest that its utility has been generally accepted.

In the tasks of nation building in transitional societies, bureaucracy has a vital role to play. It consists, by and large, of people with progressive motivation, wide administrative experience, and a rich store of pooled knowledge. Far from being written off, it cannot even be ignored. It must also be conceded that it has played an important part in the process of economic and social growth and has been willing to go at least part of the way to adjust to the new situation. It has functioned both as a model and as an instrument for modernization. But its effective utilization has been blocked by some of the paradoxes of the new political culture and by the contradictions within its own structure and in the ordering of its values. In several respects the hard core of bureaucratic culture has been unyielding, and has offered great resistance to innovation. The blame does not lie entirely at its own door but, at the same time, the present state of uncertainty cannot be allowed to continue indefinitely. The absence of an adequate understanding of its culture and values, and of a balanced assessment of its past and future roles, has been an important factor in the failure to utilize bureaucracy more effectively in programmes of economic growth and planned change.

SEVEN

Bureaucracy and Economic Development

Formal organizations are an essential attribute of modern societies. The transition from simpler forms of traditional society to increasingly complex forms of modern society necessitates a shift from a social organization based on kinship and rooted in ritual to a network of formal organizations built upon rationality, effectiveness, and efficiency. The modern State operates through a series of interacting formal organizations: bureaucracy is its principal instrument. The expansion of State activity, especially the increasing involvement of governments in economic development and technical change in the underdeveloped societies, has added to the pivotal significance of bureaucracy.

Many of the problems and tasks that the new nations are

facing today are unprecedented in magnitude and complexity. First, in most of them, the maintenance of order is a live problem. The cohesive bonds of nationhood being weak, parochial loyalties—tribal, ethnic, religious, regional, and linguistic—assert themselves from time to time in violent forms. The agitational and coercive approach to problem solving contributes significantly to unstable conditions. Second, the pressing necessity of adding measurably to the national output through the modernization of both agriculture and industry is another formidable task before them. This cannot be done by wishful thinking and exhortation; it requires effective planning and efficient implementation. The last two decades have demonstrated beyond doubt that freedom, by itself, does not provide the answers to the economic malaise of developing nations: realistic—and often hard—decisions in respect of resource mobilization and management have to be taken and supported by sustained effort to realize the output goals. Third, their cultural goals are also important. In the cultural field they appear to be pursuing unlimited utopias. Their quest for identity is beset with many contradictions, dilemmas, and paradoxes. The irreconcilable goals of nativistic revival and economic modernization are often sought to be attained simultaneously, and the competing pulls of the traditionalists and the modernizers have to be harmonized. These uneasy compromises cause severe stresses and strains and, in consequence, cultural advancement is considerably retarded.

In the pursuit of the *order*, *output*, and *cultural* goals of the State, bureaucracy can play an important role. It may merge with the authoritarian political stream and turn into a "party-State bureaucracy" or a "military-dominated bureaucracy" or a "ruler-dominated bureaucracy" and, of course, may function as a "ruling bureaucracy". But as a "representative bureaucracy", with a separate identity and clearly demarcated and delimited spheres of responsibility and authority, it can function as a stabilizing factor.[1] Although it is not without its occupational diseases, it does represent experience and expertise, and can thus contribute to the continuity of policies and provide correctives to immature political processes that are guided by sentiment and political exigencies of the moment rather than by rational calculation and long-term perspective.

ROLES OF BUREAUCRACY IN ECONOMIC DEVELOPMENT[2]

The contributions that bureaucracy can make to the process of economic development are varied and significant. First, it has to provide the minimal preconditions and basic infrastructures of economic development. Second, it has to prepare the blueprints for development and devise variable and dynamic strategies for their effective and efficient implementation. Third, it has to assess and evaluate the results of its efforts, watch their intended and unintended consequences, and ensure the evaluation and progress of its own mechanics.

The colonial bureaucracies—and also those of near-colonial countries—were trained more in the techniques of maintaining law and order than in those of nation building.

[1] For a classification of bureaucracies and for a discussion of its role in modernization see Merle Fainsod, "Bureaucracy and Modernization: The Russian and Soviet Case," in Joseph La Palombara (ed.), *Bureaucracy and Political Development*, Princeton, New Jersey, Princeton University Press, 1963.

[2] Cf. Joseph Spengler, "Bureaucracy and Economic Development," in Joseph La Palombara, *ibid.*

Their interest in economic development was peripheral and was confined mostly to *ad hoc* projects of limited duration. With the increasing emphasis that is laid today on economic development, there is a tendency to underrate bureaucracy's order maintaining functions. Law and order constitute the minimal preconditions of development, and their maintenance is, therefore, imperative for the successful implementation of plans of economic development.

Order, in the context of economic development, would also comprise at least a reasonable degree of public probity, a legal and administrative framework for economic institutions and organizations to function in, and adequate and efficient monetary and banking structures. These constitute the minimal conditions, in fact the prerequisites of the economic order and security that is necessary for economic growth.

The interdependence of order and output should be obvious to a perceptive observer. In the absence of order, the effectiveness of arrangements for economic development would be markedly reduced. On the other hand, imaginatively drawn and efficiently handled projects of economic development can materially contribute towards the reduction of stresses and tensions that lead to instability and turmoil. With conditions of relatively greater stability thus established through order oriented schemes of development, ground can be prepared for launching more comprehensive plans of economic development.

Another sphere in which bureaucracy can make an indirect but none the less significant contribution is that of providing for and maintaining the infrastructures of development. Communications, education, and health, among others, have a demonstrably meaningful bearing on the accelaration of economic growth. Particularly important are the attitude and value changes favourable to the emergence of an ideological-motivational framework which can provide a propitious setting for the acceleration of economic development. Lerner has identified empathy, mobility, and high participation as the personality attributes most conducive to modernization.[3] Communications and education can serve as effective instruments of personality change. They can break inhibitions, raise aspirations, and encourage experimentation. Careful strategies and judicious investments to build these infrastructures can be counted on to pay rich dividends by stimulating economic development. Thus, alongside the maintenance of law, order, and security, the provision and maintenance of certain key infrastructures is yet another vital field in which bureaucracy has an important role to play.

The operational mechanics of planning and development involve three basic steps: (*i*) formulation of the general goals of development, and fixation, in different sectors, of specific targets calculated to achieve the overall objectives. This is to be done within the framework of an ideology supported by as broad a consensus as possible. Of course, the serious consideration of feasibility cannot be ignored in this context; (*ii*) mobilization and management of resources geared to specific and overall, and short and long-term, objectives; (*iii*) transformation of inputs into outputs in such ways that the objectives of development would be realized.

A representative bureaucracy has inevitably to work under political direction and controls and, as such, it has little choice in determining the ideology that motivates the process

[3]Daniel Lerner, *The Passing of Traditional Society*, Glencoe, The Free Press, 1962.

of goal setting. Choices in this sphere are essentially political. However, the feasibility factor, if it is ignored beyond a limit, can immobilize ideologically inspired objectives of a utopian nature. The political elite often points out what *should* be done; the bureaucracy, on the other hand, is in a position to indicate what *can* be done. An understanding political administrator would not disregard lightly the advice and warnings of bureaucracy in this respect. And clearly, bureaucracy, with its experience and expertise, would have the upper hand in determining the detailed sector-wise break-up of targets.

Operationally, the other two steps go together; here the bureaucracy, as the principal arm of the political executive, has considerable leeway. Resource surveys as well as the mobilization and management of resources are largely in the hands of the bureaucracy. The blueprints for development, although they are guided by ideology, are prepared largely on the basis of the findings of the resource surveys. The manipulation of resources, human and natural, towards the attainment of specified ends is the task of bureaucracy. Thus, bureaucracy is responsible for much of the mechanics of actual planning, including perspective planning, and also for the detailed executive handling of the plans. With its insights and trained human resources, it can make a meaningful contribution to both. Both require dynamic and variable strategies.

Most developing societies have mixed economies with more or less clearly demarcated *private* and *public* sectors, and there is often also a third sector—a *people's* sector, especially in the rural areas—where partnership projects like community development are run jointly by the people and the government. These three spheres require the direct involvement of bureaucracy. First, bureaucracy has to perform regulatory functions in relation to the private sector. Second, it has directly to operate the public sector. Third, it has to handle partnership programmes like the community development projects.

Two more functions of bureaucracy merit special mention. Inter-sectoral co-ordination is its special charge, and it has a processing function in the communications network. The balancing of projects in the three sectors and the co-ordination of programmes ramifying from one sector into another require expert handling. In the processing of communication also bureaucracy is a key factor. While it is true that the four human components in the communications network—the party in power, the bureaucracy, the elites, and the masses—have direct links with one another, the day-to-day executive role of bureaucracy gives its processing function here an added significance.

Finally, concurrent and periodic appraisal of the progress of plans is necessary. Concurrent evaluation may be done by an administrative agency itself or this responsibility may be assigned to an independent organization. A mechanism for concurrent evaluation built into the administrative machinery is often found useful. Experts from outside can be associated with *ad hoc* assessments at regular intervals. A sincerely motivated bureaucracy is not reluctant to do some serious heart-searching, and should not be sensitive to its failures being pointed out by others. Timely correctives can be provided as a result. A special effort can be made to see if the intended results are being produced. At the same time, attempts should be made to look for unintended consequences of a dysfunctional and injurious nature: strategies to counteract these will save the plans from misdirection. In sum, the remedial measures thrown up by appraisal, assessment, and evaluation will contribute to the evolution of the system of developmental administration along progressive lines, and will keep it in harness for meeting new challenges.

PATHOLOGIES AND DYSFUNCTIONS

Max Weber, the master theoretician of bureaucracy, found in it four attributes that marked it out for its advantages. It was *efficient*, *predictable*, *impersonal*, and *fast*. As an ideal type it could possess all these attributes and perhaps more, but the sociological analysis of its functioning in transitional societies shows that, in fact, it is not so. Recent researches have brought to light some of its pathologies and dysfunctions. Because of its training (more particularly because of the allocation of its personnel to narrow specialities) and its use of time-tested methods, it can be efficient, but these very factors impart to it what Veblen would call a *trained incapacity* to handle new situations. As bureaucracy follows categorical rules and principles, its course of action can be predicted with a high degree of accuracy. But a close analysis of its functioning would reveal that in the course of its action there is considerable goal displacement, which severely limits the element of predictability. Bureaucracy can be impersonal in a soulless kind of way, but the human element plays a significant part in its inner dynamics and detracts from its impersonal character. It is well known that informal organizations exist within formal organizations and play a not unimportant role. As for the last attribute, its speed, jokes about its immobility are legion. A prisoner of its own procedures, in uncharted territories it often crawls at a snail's pace. These pathologies and dysfunctions are perhaps nowhere more evident than in the still largely unexplored regions of economic development.

THE INDIAN CASE

India has been fortunate to inherit from the British a first class civil service tradition. Notwithstanding the fact that the Indian bureaucracy also suffers from the pathologies and dysfunctions noted above, its positive contributions to the country in the first two decades of freedom remain insufficiently acknowledged. It has had to face a barrage of criticism—much of it unjustified—and the compliments given to it have rarely been without reservations. A word of honest praise for its role in facing horrendous situations efficiently, in maintaining a degree of national cohesion, and in putting on its feet a nation-wide programme of economic development is its rightful due.

In tasks connected with economic development, however, the Indian bureaucracy has been hesitant and unsure, and its performance and levels of achievement have not equalled its reputation. Its structure and ethos suited it more for the maintenance of law and order than for massive nation-building. Its adaptation to the emerging milieu has been beset with organizational incompatibilities, psychological resistances, and value conflicts. In consequence, it suffers from certain lags and finds itself unable to face the new challenges with ease and confidence. There is, no doubt, some evidence of adaptation, adjustment, and accommodation; on the whole, however, the situation is still largely fluid.

Take for example the generalist tradition and the paternal-authoritarian tenor of administration. In the past both these elements unmistakably contributed to the efficiency of the bureaucracy, but in the context of the contemporary situation they have become dysfunctional. The generalist's trained incapacity seriously limits his effective participation in activities connected with economic development. Planning requires a background and insight that he lacks and, being trained to work at certain levels as a superior rather than as an equal, he cannot get along with technocrats whose collaboration in this task is indispensable. The paternal-authoritarian approach has so conditioned him mentally that he cannot run partnership projects in their intended and overtly articulated spirit. Lacking specialized entrepreneurial and management training, he uses general administration techniques in the regulation of the private sector and in the running of the public sector, sometimes with comic results. His evaluative perspectives and skills, again, are limited. He is reasonably well trained for job assessments and performance audits, but lacks theoretical insights and methodological sophistication to make meaningful qualitative assessments of emerging trends, of unintended consequences, and of the long-term results of developmental projects. Under multiple political pressures, especially in conditions where he is to work under political bosses unused to administrative traditions and not immune to party pressures; his efficiency is put to a severe test. Exceptions notwithstanding, many members of bureaucracy tend to lose their nerve and to demonstrate pathological indecision and lack of innovativeness. The major symptoms of the malady are: failure to take decisions at the appropriate level, passing the buck, roping others into decision making, equivocal recommendations, anticipating what the boss wants, rationalization of failures, underplaying the essential and magnifying the grandiose, covering the failure of small utopias with projections of larger ones, and outright sycophancy.

Enough has been said to support the argument that, in the transitional setting of India, bureaucracy has not been able to function efficiently in the sphere of economic development. Many of these factors are responsible also for distracting it from its other ideal type attributes of predictability, impersonal character, and speed. Generalized objectives of development have to be broken down operationally into specific departmental projects. In the process there is considerable goal redefinition and goal displacement. Objectives as defined and articulated by particular departments—or ministers—are often at great variance with the more generalized objectives determined by the top planners. The direction that they may take in the process of redefinition is not predictable. Parochial loyalties and political pressures make the observance of categorical rules and principles difficult, adding to the unpredictability of bureaucracy's course of action. The interplay of human factors and subservience to the sovereignty of politics make significant dents in the impersonal character of the bureaucracy. Finally, bureaucracy cannot be fast because it has to operate under a dual set of procedural norms. Old procedures are cumbersome and ponderous, and the interminable journeys of files and cases from level to level and from department to department are necessarily time consuming. At the same time, new norms calling for speed and despatch are still amorphous and, therefore, uncertain.

Indian bureaucracy has always had some corruption and nepotism. Today these are on the increase. The general erosion of public morality has imparted a measure of legitimacy to them. In consequence, bureaucracy's credibility is being lowered rapidly.

DIRECTIONS OF REFORM

Social science is essentially analytic. As such, those concerned with administrative reforms will have to draw their own conclusions from sociological analyses. A few general observations on the directions in which reform may take place, however, can be made.

First, it would be idle to visualize any meaningful administrative reforms without at the same time effecting necessary political reforms. So long as political corruption exists, bureaucratic corruption will accompany it. Bureaucracy will always be vulnerable to political pressure and, as such, norms will have to be evolved which prohibit the interference of members of the Central and State legislatures and that of other political workers in day-to-day administration. At the same time, provision will have to be made to protect officials from penalties imposed on them because of their failure to accede to the unreasonable demands of the politicians. It can be stated axiomatically that a first rate administrative structure cannot evolve under a political structure that continues to be arrogant, immature, interfering, and bullying.

Second, the relationship between the political and the permanent executives needs to be re-examined and sharply defined. Non-interference in the legitimate sphere of bureaucracy's work must be assured, and its initiative and innovativeness should be strengthened by support from the political executive. The factors leading to bureaucracy's refusal to undertake responsibility should be analyzed, and necessary correctives devised.

Third, through careful reorganization and better training the structural incompatibilities of, and the value conflicts in bureaucracy should be eradicated. The generalist has had his day: diversification and specialization of cadres, especially for the tasks of economic development, is indicated as the need of the hour. Specialized training in entrepreneurial and management skills and in human relations will have to be imparted to cadres involved in economic development.

Fourth, there should be a reorientation of elite administrative cadres in two directions—they should be better sensitized to the socio-political climate and the cultural ethos in which they will have to function, and conscious efforts should be made to inculcate in them qualities of interactive rather than authoritarian leadership.

Fifth, rather than pay only lip service to the criterion of merit, the administration will have to devise objective indicators of merit to guide the selection and promotion of cadres.

Sixth, a systematic and ongoing programme of imaginatively drawn studies of the processes of public administration will have to be instituted to detect pathologies and dysfunctions, so that necessary correctives to them may be devised.

In his novel, *The Civil Service*, Balzac referred to bureaucracy as "a gigantic power manipulated by dwarfs". Emerging nations can ill afford to let this definition be true in their case.

EIGHT

Modernization and Education

The complex processes of modernization assume a series of interpenetrating and interdependent transformations. On the level of personality, it is now widely recognized, they envisage characterological changes resulting in the promotion of rationality, empathy, mobility, and high participation. These attributes of the modernized personality are promoted and sustained by—and, in their turn, promote and sustain—institutional and value change on the social and cultural levels. The social and cultural milieu, thus, increasingly aquires achievemental, universalistic, and specificity oriented emphases. It accepts and produces more innovations, builds up associational capability, and sharpens its problem solving abilities. Absence of fit between the modernized personality and the social/cultural framework would lead to an uncomfortable imbalance. For this reason harmonization and interlinking of the changes in the personality, cultural, and social systems is essential. In the context of modernization these transformations must be viewed as preconditions to the growth of complex organizations that can adequately and effectively exploit and manipulate energy from inanimate sources for human well-being and prosperity.

Three assumptions are basic to this conception of modernization; (*i*) inanimate sources of power must be tapped increasingly to solve human problems and to ensure a minimal acceptable standard of living, the ceiling of which is progressively rising; (*ii*) this can be done best by collective rather than individual effort; associational capability to operate through increasingly complex organizations is thus a prerequisite to at least the middle and higher reaches of modernization; (*iii*) such complex organizations cannot be created and run without radical personality change and attendant changes in the social structures and in the cultural fabric.

No techniques are known to achieve an instant switch from the stone axe to the steam engine. Man's technological progress has been slow and tortuous: some groups progressed more because of their propitious ecological, cultural, and motivational settings, others could at first assimilate and adopt the new technology only in limited doses and later made efforts to develop it independently, while still others could accept only its products without being able to master the intricacies of its organization and techniques. The last category, now an aspirant to modernized status, constitutes two-thirds of mankind. Far from being able to take the road to creative innovation, many of these societies are not yet ready even for transfer or adaptation of modern technology. This is accounted for partly by their attitudinal and institutional inadequacies, and partly also by their lack of associational capability. They have the desire to enjoy the fruits of modernization, but their institutional, organizational, and ideological-motivational framework is not ready yet to adopt modern technology on a large scale. They also lack the infrastructure to adapt foreign technology to their peculiar needs and to innovate in the modern style to meet the challenge of the revolution of rising expectations.

A sound strategy for modernization would appear to include: (*i*) directed change in the system of attitudes, beliefs and values, and also in the institutional complex, to enhance the acceptability of modern technology and its organizational and operational framework; (*ii*) growth of the infrastructure essential to the adaptation of technology of foreign origin to specific national needs; (*iii*) laying the foundations of institutions and organizations which could, in time, assume responsibility for independent innovation and technological growth relevant to the country's needs and problems.

Undeniably, education can be a most potent instrument of modernization. Directly, it seeks to promote knowledge and to develop skills, both essential for the furtherance of the goals of modernization. At the same time some of its indirect consequences, such as value and attitude change, are also not without significance. The priority accorded to education in programmes of modernization is, thus, not misplaced. How effectively it is organized and how well it is directed is a different matter.

Some of the ways in which education is functional to the programmes of modernization have been identified.

By enlarging the cognitive map of those exposed to it,

education suggests alternatives to tradition, brings into focus the rewards implicit in them, and indicates—roughly, at least—the paths through which the new goals with their attendant rewards can be achieved. It broadens mental horizons, raises expectations, and predisposes people to make experiments.

As an instrument of socialization it can project new images and values. Purposively used, it can be a help in obliterating attitudes and behaviour patterns that are dysfunctional to programmes of modernization.

By providing ideological articulation it can promote the feeling of nationhood and can help people see their needs and problems in a national perspective. This can stimulate the creation of a national consensus, at least on major issues.

Education provides a highway to elite status. It is not the only avenue through which personnel to the elite ranks is recruited, but there is perhaps no developing society which does not confer a special status on the educated. The educated provide a reference model to the masses who take their first steps away from tradition in imitation of the former. Modernizing elites are almost always the products of modern or semi-modern school/university systems.

Problem solving leadership—scientists and technicians, management experts, and administrators—with requisite knowledge and skills can be expected to emerge only from the educational system. Large-scale programmes of modernization demand specialists of several types at different levels; it is the educational system that provides a steady flow of technocrats, planners, and managers to operate them.

Education is a mobility multiplier. Although its initial impact is on the immobility of ways of thinking, in the long run it does alter rigid forms of social stratification.

Modernization requires both types of mobility.

In sum, with proper planning and under efficient direction, education can make a meaningful contribution to the attainment of modernization. It can be harnessed to diffuse the attitudes and ideologies required for the adoption of modern technology and its associated values and organizational premises, to provide the personnel to operate and sustain the programmes of modernization, and to create capabilities for the adaptation and origination of new technology.

But education is only an instrument, and an instrument, in the final analysis, is only as good as the person wielding it. The efficacy of education as an instrument of modernization would depend largely on its orientation and content as well as on those who impart and receive it. In fact, it is a two-edged weapon: it can serve the aims of the traditionalists just as well as it can serve the aims of the modernizers. Under certain conditions, by generating stresses and strains, it may even produce anomic disturbances that are difficult to control and that obstruct ordered movement towards modernity. Therefore, it would be useful to bear in mind some of its dysfunctional aspects as well.

By enlarging the cognitive map, education redefines and resets cultural goals. Up to a point this is necessary and is functional. But cultural goals must bear some relationship to institutional means. Education often becomes dysfunctional when it sets cultural goals way beyond the institutional means of a society. Inadequacy of the institutional set-up results in anger and frustration, and later in defiance and destruction.

While education can project new images and help the inculcation of new values, it can also be turned into an instrument for the perpetuation of traditional values that may run counter to the objectives of modernization. Education does not produce only modernizers, it produces traditionalists also. And some of these traditionalists-by-choice are incomparably more articulate and sophisticated than those who may be called "traditionalists who know nothing different".

Several types of traditionalists can be identified: (*i*) those with whom tradition is a habit of mind because they know nothing better or even different, and whose naive and simplistic traditionalism stands apart as a category by itself; (*ii*) those with a highly selective perception, who identify their culture with its past high achievement in particular fields, ignoring harsh and inconvenient empirical realities, both ancient and contemporary; (*iii*) the cultural narcissists with unbounded and undiscriminating nostalgia for the past, who find in tradition a compensation for what the society lacks (or is denied) today; (*iv*) those with whom traditionalism is a pose, a mask, and a carefully cultivated style, and who want to stand out from the rest: this category includes also those to whom traditionalism is a convenient political gimmick; (*v*) those who have a vested interest in tradition and who remain attached to it because of their benefits derived from it; and (*vi*) pragmatic traditionalists, who are afraid of the uncertainties of modernization and associate it with some of the ills of the contemporary world.

Traditionalists of the last five categories can easily superimpose their value-attitude systems on education. For political reasons they may even consciously feed the irrational beliefs of the first category. Education, thus, may promote conflicting goals.

Because of the simultaneous operation of push and pull factors in education, both centrifugal and centripetal forces may be promoted at the same time. Ideological contradictions in the content of education may weaken the feeling of nation-ness and consensus by lending at least partial support to parochialism.

Education is undeniably an avenue to status, but when it fails to maintain a feasible want-get ratio it also results in status denial to many who feel entitled to, and qualified for, it. It may create status aspirations that do not take account of society's needs and the aspirant's talents and abilities.

The foreign models and idiom of education often produce academic and scientific styles that fail to see problems in the perspective of national needs. International styles—including current fashions and even fads—are blindly imitated even though their relevance to national problems is doubtful or patently useless. Intellectual activity, thus, runs the risk of degenerating into barren exercises in futility. Problem solving objectives may get blurred and blunted.

Vested interests may often seek to utilize education to maintain and sustain traditional forms of stratification. In many cases it may actually widen the gap between classes and between different social categories.

When education gets to be viewed as an end in itself rather than as a means to certain objectives, it becomes an article of consumption; the costs involved in this are considerable. The scarce resources invested on it could be more meaningfully utilized in other sectors of economic growth.

Management of the educational explosion is often difficult. The stresses and strains built into the system result in the production of highly volatile and inflammable material that may add to the corpus of problems rather than contribute to their solution.

It is, thus, evident that education with inept handling can put societies in reverse motion. The dangers to be guarded against most are: education becoming an instrument of traditionalism; education raising hopes and aspirations whose fulfilment is not immediately feasible and practical; education attaining aims and purposes unrelated to modernization and often pulling in the opposite direction; and education creating pervasive discontent and anomic conditions that retard progress towards modernization.

Strategies of educational planning for modernization are beset with several unresolved dilemmas—national need versus "social justice" or expanded opportunity; quality versus quantity; strategic and selective planning versus operation of market laws of demand and supply; *good* education for *some* versus *some* education for *all*; and consumption-orientation versus production-orientation in education. All too often scarce resources are thinly spread, the development of needed skills is subordinated to the requirements of diffused consumption-type education dictated by popular pressure, and substandard teachers working in substandard institutions turn out substandard products. Thus the potential of education for modernization is rarely exploited in full measure. Unless these dilemmas are satisfactorily resolved, it is doubtful if education can make its proper contribution to modernization. It needs focus, direction and, above all, relevance.

NINE

Indian Universities: The Crisis Within

Higher education is expanding at a very rapid pace in India. In 1947 there were only twenty universities in the country; today there are seventy. In addition to these, ten institutions are "deemed" to be universities and are empowered to grant their own degrees. There are strong regional pressures for the creation of still more universities, and several established as well as new institutions are clamouring for degree-conferring status. In spite of the University Grants Commission's sane advice to the States to go slow in this matter, new universities are coming up and will continue to come up. With cautious forethought, careful planning, and sound management, the inputs in this educational adventure could have become profitable investments in the country's programme of modernization; but, because of the casual and thoughtless manner in which older universities are run and new ones set up, university education appears to have become only an item of prestigious consumption. The scarce resources that should have gone into qualitative growth go instead into avoidable duplication of mediocre institutions offering irrelevant, out of date, and uninspiring instruction, and producing annual crops of degree holders most of whom qualify for nothing in particular.

There is pervasive discontent in universities. Institutions that should have been peaceful temples of learning are today in turmoil and live from crisis to crisis. Those involved in financing and running them, and in benefiting from them—politicians in and out of power, academic administrators, the faculty, and the students—look at universities wearing glasses with different tints. Each of these elements has a different conception of the aim of a university and each prescribes a different remedy for its ills. The result is confusion. All too often, the crises in the university are attributed to "student indiscipline". No effort is made to look searchingly for the structural inadequacies and incompatibilities, and the conceptual imbalances and contradictions in the university system that have made a mess of higher education in the country.

Many of the older universities—built on a model that was a mixture of Oxbridge and London—are no longer on the high pedestals that they occupied in the years of their glory. Constant political interference, recurrent financial deficits, unimaginative and ineffective management, absence of courageous innovations, intra-faculty politics, and inability to handle student unrest appear to have paralyzed them. They embody concepts and offer academic programmes that are several decades out of date and are wholly out of tune with the changed social milieu. They have not been able to cope with the contemporary explosion of knowledge. They are sick in body and soul, and cannot be either pace-setters for desired progress or models for new universities. The new universities—with the exception of the Institutes of Technology and some agricultural universities—can be regarded as "new" only in respect of the dates of their establishment; in other respects they are pale carbon copies of the older and more established universities. Architecturally most of them are ugly, and academically they are dull and uninspiring. Set up with considerable fanfare in response to popular demand (or with an eye on political gains) they are generally neglected and allowed to languish. Many of them are no more than examination offices dignified with the title of "university". It is amazing that even the universities set up in the late sixties in this country do not reflect any of the powerful currents of contemporary thinking on higher education. It is not surprising that most of them are intellectually sterile.

The seats of power that take decisions about universities—old and new—appear to be blissfully ignorant of the concept of the modern university and of its role in meeting the challenges of the future. It is doubtful if they even make any meaningful distinction between an ordinary college and a university. The poor financial allocations that they make for the universities expose their lack of awareness of a university's requirements in coping with the explosion of knowledge—which doubles itself in a decade—and of extending the frontiers of the disciplines it encompasses. Appointments to the office of Vice-Chancellor are often matters of political patronage. Invariably, only safe and compliant individuals are appointed to this much devalued office. There is constant political interference even in the matter of academic promotions and new appointments. Academically oriented Vice-Chancellors who stand for autonomy and progressive policies are dealt with in a variety of ways. University Acts are modified to ease them out of office. If this is somehow stalled (through court decisions or otherwise), funds are denied to the university in order to teach its Vice-Chancellor a lesson. Even cruder methods are not barred. The support of student activists is mobilized to inconvenience the Vice-Chancellor. In the faculty itself some members can usually be found who willingly oppose and subvert the progressive policies of the Vice-Chancellor. Few politicians and political parties can resist the temptation to fish in the troubled waters of a university for short-term personal and political gains. There is a distinct trend to increase governmental control over universities. A study of recent legislation in respect of universities would be instructive. Analysis of the role of politicians in university affairs would also be extremely revealing.

Academic administrators endowed with vision, dynamism, and the management skills that are necessary for the growth of institutions which can take up the challenge of modern education are difficult to find. Even the most dynamic among Vice-Chancellors have found it difficult to resist pressures from without and from within. But most of them owe their assignment to political patronage and are content to carry out the bidding of their masters. To avoid trouble they surrender easily to the power of internal blackmail as well. They and their henchmen have little appreciation of the idiom of modern scholarship and of the prerequisites and infrastructures of productive research. The administration is either stiflingly authoritarian or too weak to be effective. In either case, it is insensitive to the demands of creativity and is incapable of responding adequately to the challenge of ever-expanding frontiers of knowledge. In this process, teaching and research turn into monotonous routine and meaningless ritual. Those who enter university for the adventures of ideas get frustrated, for they are often reduced to the position of helpless witnesses of drift and futility. Some of them seek avenues of adequate expression abroad, some give up and learn to conform after a few ineffective protests, and a few retire into self-created shells and continue doing whatever little they can in the unwholesome and unpropitious academic climate.

The situation would not have deteriorated so much had university faculties been alert, articulate, and responsive to the changing needs of society. From year to year the condition has been worsening for a variety of reasons. There is a lot of dead wood in the universities, and there are no known ways of getting rid of it. There is a sizable section of honest and intellectually motivated teachers, but they do not have proper guidance and leadership. At every step they have to encounter the power of negative thinking. The university system, they find, has built-in mechanisms to frustrate genuine intellectual quests. Some of the better known of the distinguished teachers are oriented more to M.I.T., Harvard, Oxford, and Cambridge than to their own country and their own universities. No effective programmes of faculty development are devised and little attention is given to the exploitation of the full potential of able young colleagues. Many of those occupying the higher reaches of the power pyramid in different disciplines are preoccupied with endless meetings of committees, boards, and seminars, and with distributing largess to their tail-wagging admirers and supporters. An incredible degree of sycophancy prevails in these academic establishments. In consequence, charlatans and academic chameleons are often favoured in preference to men of solid academic worth in making university appointments and promotions. Little attention is given to the pressing problems of curricula modernization and reform in methods of instruction and examination. Perceptive and able teachers soon discover the hollowness of their leaders, but there is little they can do to make themselves heard. These small establishments are so entrenched in the larger ones that the dissident is either ignored or dismissed as an oddball.

The students are unwitting victims of the prevailing academic confusion, and they also add to it in ample measure. Products of a faulty school system, they get bewildered in the many cultures that coexist within the university. Many of them are inadequately prepared for higher education. Instruction through a foreign language which was never taught to them properly, monotonous lectures on topics whose relevance to contemporary life is never brought home to them, and the uninspiring personal examples of their mentors are not conducive to the pursuit of excellence. They soon learn that agitation rather than request is the more effective way of securing redressal of their legitimate grievances. The attitude of the authorities towards them swings between apathy and indulgence. They are first neglected to the point of desperation and revolt; then, to soothe their violent temper, the authorities make one concession after another. Apart from lowering academic standards, these concessions inflate the ego of the "activists", who become a law unto themselves and paralyze the life of the university from time to time just to make sure that their importance is duly recognized. Little effort is made to put the energies of the students into constructive channels.

That there is a crisis within the university system is widely accepted, but its magnitude and dimensions are not sufficiently recognized. Notwithstanding an endless succession of commissions, study groups, and panels, and their platitudinous reports—containing also some sound advice—the situation has become steadily worse. No purposeful action has been taken to give a focus and an aim to the universities. The Kothari Commission's report—admirable in many respects—is gathering dust and will perhaps meet the fate of its predecessors. The fate of many useful schemes emanating from the U.G.C. was no better. Suggestions for change without guidance in its management are not enough. The U.G.C. does not seem to recognize this. But the U.G.C., over the years, has become a slow-moving giant monolithic structure; its intricate procedures, bureaucratic routine, and establishment oriented outlook are not conducive to dynamic action.

The malady afflicting Indian universities is more widespread and malignant than we care to admit today. The evil effects of the present neglect and inaction will be apparent a decade or two later. To save the situation we must act now.

TEN

The Restive Students

The explosive situation in the college and university campuses of India has assumed truly disturbing proportions. The first murmurs of unease had become audible a decade ago, but their potential for large-scale anomic disturbances remained unrecognized. Superficial diagnoses, coupled with unimaginative and ineffective handling, allowed them to grow into loud and vociferous protests. Educational planners and administrators had grudgingly to take note of them, but the true import of the developing situation was lost in a flood of easy and often false rationalizations. These protests were treated as individual episodes in the deteriorating law and order situation: the handling of the students wavered between apathy and indulgence, and rarely was the challenge met with resolute and purposeful action. Verbal protests made way for open defiance of authority, for violence, and for acts that according to the canons of civilized society can only be described as criminal. Today we have reached a point where authorities are throwing up their hands in despair and the crisis-resolving mechanisms appear to have been knocked out of gear. Even the most cursory glance at the newspapers convincingly brings home to us the point that our educational institutions live from crisis to crisis, and their authorities are all too often willing to go down on the knees and offer fantastic concessions and incredible prices to buy temporary—and often illusory—peace on the campuses.

Here I propose to identify the major strands and themes in the contemporary youth culture of India. It is common to speak of "Indian students" or "contemporary youth" as an undifferentiated mass. This is a mistake, for the differences in background, orientation, and outlook are many and significant. The subcultures of contemporary youth present variations not only of idiom and style, but also of goals and instrumentalities.

The imitation *flower children*, the Indian counterparts of the hippies, can be dismissed as a temporary aberration. A product of the permissiveness of the urban upper class, they exploit its indulgence to experiment furtively with pot or the occasional shot. They carry all the symbols of hippiedom, but not its philosophy: their consciously cultivated outlandish and bizarre dress, manner, and speech represent at best a protest against parental authority. They never really question the foundations of the social order seriously. Treated with amused tolerance, most of these spurious hippies outgrow their adolescent rebellion and revert to conformity. They rarely pose a threat to the educational system except, perhaps, as a distracting model.

The *mods* constitute another category, slightly more numerous, and slightly more problematic. These children of affluence belong to a distinct cultural world: the world of discotheques and their pop music and dancing, of the compulsive high fashion diffused in a subtle and suggestive manner by the mass media, and of the mad merry-go-round of parties with all the latest frills and trimmings. They are a special case of bohemianism, playing it "hot" or "cool" according to the fashion of the day, always trying to be "with it". This westernized and alienated set has little in common with the mainstream of Indian life but, curiously, many of these self-styled modernists accept some of the superstitions and much of the ritual of tradition. This rather small group is confined largely to metropolitan centres. Its members generally keep to themselves, not mingling either with the more populous groups of *trads*, i.e., the *behnjis* and the *bhaijis*, or with what they regard as the "trash" from the urban slums and the "riffraff" from the villages, with all of whom they have to share campus life and privileges. By and large, they keep away from campus politics also. A few of them possibly develop serious intellectual motivation, but to many the academic routine is oriented more to the acquisition of the magic alphabets—B.A. or B.Sc., M.A. or M.Sc.—than to the cultivation of the spirit of inquiry. Most of them count on their parents' contacts and influence to find remunerative positions. On a section of the other students their influence is unwholesome. Those so influenced by them are the less affluent, who weave a make believe world around themselves on the model of this swinging set and pathetically try to emulate their style, but the meagre resources of whose parents cannot afford this luxury.

A third and relatively large group has its origins in the medium-to-low-privilege strata of society who nevertheless have a background of literacy. University education gets high priority in their planning for life. They hope that it will give them an upward push in the status ladder; at any rate, education is a must if they are to maintain their precarious social position. A high percentage of serious minded and diligent students comes from this group. Their transition from the culture of the home to the culture of the school and then on to the culture of the university is relatively smooth. The career-oriented section among them generally tends to conform and seeks the benefits of the university system, its inadequacies notwithstanding. A section develops indifference and carries on the academic routine as a kind of ritual. But among them there is a section also of those who look questioningly at the social order and its academic arm—the college and the university system. Those who dissent, those who resent, and those who rebel are thrown up by this section. A small but articulate fraction of the leadership of contemporary youth comes from this source.

The fourth group, by far the largest, consists of first generation literates and those whose parents did not have the benefit of higher education. The urban lower classes and the rural masses contribute this sizable group. The absence of fit between the culture of the home and the neighbourhood on the one hand, and the culture of the school on the other is, in their case, glaring. Even at the school stage they develop a measure of alienation from the parental culture. Not many of them are intellectually and emotionally prepared to enter the portals of institutions of higher learning. The transition from home to school results in cultural dissonance, but some of the constraints of the elders' authority persist. The transition from the school to the university, with no cushioning provided, is often traumatic. Many derive their image of university life from popular fiction and glossy films—a life of little responsibility, of more play than disciplined work. Often the teacher is portrayed as a genial buffoon whose antics add comic relief to their rounds of gaiety and romance. The school system does little to correct this distorted image.

But there are also those who enter upon their university careers with a genuine quest—a will to learn. The shreds and patches of information they have picked up at school, they find to their dismay, are no preparation for the pursuit of higher knowledge and academic excellence. If the school system did not mould them to the requirements of the university, the universities themselves have done little to adapt to the needs of the new entrants. Some of these students are distracted by glittering non-academic pursuits, but even the seekers find in the inflexible and sterile university system little to inspire or stimulate them. Some become indifferent and stay indifferent; others learn to articulate their resentment; some graduate into open defiance and revolt. The unorganized majority wavers between ritualistic conformity and indifference; the organized minority crystallizes dissent and spearheads the revolt. In the concrete manifestations of revolt trivial and non-academic objectives get so inextricably mixed up with higher revolutionary aims that it becomes difficult to categorize the student leadership either as new revolutionaries or as hooligans on the rampage.

To sum up, what kind of a configuration do we get of the culture or cultures of contemporary youth in India? Some themes are common and recurrent. First, disenchantment with the social order and the establishment is growing. Some would like to tear it down for they find no hope in it; others, not without hope, would not go so far, but even they want more performance than promise. There is also a distinct awareness that the generation of elders has failed them and that the future is fraught with uncertainty. Second, the legitimacy of the politics of pressure and protest if not of violence is being increasingly conceded. Third, a feeling is gradually crystallizing that the university system is sterile and non-functional, if not entirely irrelevant, to the contemporary needs of India. It lacks innovativeness, dynamism, and adaptability. Fourth, there is a heightened awareness of youth power; that they have a cause is recognized, but in regard to its content and the direction of the struggle to achieve it there is no unanimity.

Beyond these we are confronted with a set of contradictions and contrary pulls. While some face westward for their ideology and socio-political models, others seek them from rival capitals of world revolution, some others want a home-spun brand of socialism, and still others would go in for the revival of tradition and would discard both foreign ideologies and their indigenous adaptations. Even young radicals wanting to usher in a new social order based on equality do not hesitate to use caste as an operative principle in their politics. The elders are criticized and rejected for their politics, but in practice the critics themselves adopt the same political style. Considerations of power and glory often outweigh considerations of common good. There is no unanimity on the aims and the desired content of higher education. On methods of remedying its ills also there is wide divergence of opinion. On these issues the youth movement remains divided, and the ferment continues.

SYMPTOMS AND DIAGNOSES

From all indications the tide of student unrest is rising and the efforts to contain it have not been very successful. Eighty-five campus incidents and agitations were reported in one or more of eight newspapers with an all-India circulation that were surveyed in 1968 by a major national agency involved in the development of higher education in the country. Figures for 1969, based on reports in the same newspapers, are strikingly higher. That year two hundred and sixty-one incidents—brief or protracted—merited reporting in the columns of these newspapers, registering a 207 per cent increase over the last year. Admittedly this is not the most satisfactory way of measuring student unrest or of analyzing its trends, but in the absence of fuller and more analytical treatment of campus happenings, it provides a basis for drawing some conclusions broadly indicative of the prevailing situation.

To get back to the newspaper coverage. In 1968, 53 per cent of the incidents were related to campus issues and the rest, i.e., 47 per cent, were connected with off-campus issues. No agitations and strikes were reported from thirty-eight universities. In 1969, trouble spread to some of these relatively peaceful campuses also, and its volume was considerably larger. But more dramatic than the quantitative increase was a qualitative change in their character. Altogether, eighty-nine incidents that year were connected with campus issues, registering a 98 per cent increase over comparable incidents in 1968. The increase in troubles over off-campus issues was 330 per cent. In all a hundred and seventy-two cases of this type were reported. The shift definitely was towards agitation over off-campus issues. In 1968 they accounted for 47 per cent of all reported incidents; in 1969 they went up to 66 per cent. The happenings of 1968 appear tame when compared to the stubborn defiance and the calculated violence displayed in the unhappy occurrences of 1969. The years that followed were more crisis-ridden and troubled. There was evidence of much greater hardline activism. Incidents were no longer sporadic and violence was much more intense.

The distinction between *campus issues* and *off-campus issues,* it should be admitted, is somewhat artificial. Most of the charters of student demands make puzzling reading, for they represent a curious amalgam of lofty revolutionary goals and trivial parochial concerns.

Campus issues include minor irritants and lack of facilities, standards and procedures of admissions and examinations, and the ideas of student participation and joint governance of universities. Trivial-looking problems, when allowed to pile up, cause a great deal of annoyance and frustration. University management has not given much evidence of foresight, imagination, and initiative in anticipatory handling of these problems. An unfortunate impression has gained ground among the students that authorities respond only to the language of agitation and the idiom of violence. The debate among the elders on some of the key issues involved has been ponderous and inconclusive; corrective measures have been late, half-hearted, and inadequate. Student activists can claim credit for forcing some serious rethinking on the question of equalizing educational opportunity and on the issue of medium of instruction. But towards the raising of academic standards and the cultivation of excellence their movement has taken a somewhat negative attitude. If anything, the demand has been for lowering examination standards. No concerted movement has been launched for the modernization of curricula and for the introduction of challenging courses relevant to the changing world. There has been no protest against the trite and time-worn lecture method of instruction. By and large, innovations and reforms have been resisted by the students. Nor have the students organized any *teach-ins* to widen and sharpen their awareness of the forces that are shaping the contemporary world. University youth have been far too undemanding of their teachers.

The off-campus issues that have led to conflict are many and varied. They encompass problems as diverse as "world peace" and "equality of man" on the one hand and cinema concessions and free transport on the other. Bleak prospects of employment have agitated the minds of many, and have drawn even the more serious minded students of professional and technological institutions into the chorus of protest. Agitations for regional and subregional causes, such as the location of public sector enterprises and the creation of separate States, derive at least partly from this concern. The language controversy is not just a matter of sentiment or an instrument of politics, but has an economic aspect also.

Many students join the agitations and struggles out of an urge to participate in national affairs and to build for themselves and for the country a future approximating their conception of the desirable and the ideal. But a sizable group among them unwittingly falls prey to the power game of some of the elders, who deftly turn its revolutionary urge to parochial causes. Thus we have the paradox of new revolutionaries championing narrow, local, and sectarian issues that may temporarily serve the interests of a party or a faction but do no service to the nation. And we have to admit with some regret that a number of these agitations, involving arson and damage to public property, are engineered by student leaders with the covert objective of demonstrating their power and maintaining their glory. Some of them do so with an eye on their own political future.

In retrospect, two basic motivations appear to underlie the current restiveness of university youth. First, an urge to establish a different and an adult identity. Second, a desire to work for the improvement of the human condition both at home and abroad.

The spirit of revolt is not to be deprecated. In fact, youth will be found wanting in an essential ingredient if they lack it. But the revolutionary urge becomes self-defeating when it ends up in a series of unsettling disturbances, taking society backward rather than forward in the process. While major social evils and economic injustices remain to be fought, it is pathetic to find students using up their energy for trivial causes. Adults have a role in channelizing the energy and the revolutionary urges of the young, but it is mainly for the youth to rethink their aims and strategies.

In differentiated and complex societies, the young have a tendency to build a contra-culture of their own which has a series of norms and values opposed to those of the larger society. It can express itself in rebellion of three different forms—delinquency, bohemianism, or radicalism. Delinquency encompasses aggressiveness, celebration of prowess, and seeking and receiving material rewards. Bohemianism can wear many garbs, and its fads and styles change with time. Radicalism also manifests itself in many different forms: one of them involves the vision of the apocalypse—the view that the evil world of temptations and corruptions will eventually be replaced by a purer and a better one; it may also express itself in populism—belief in the creative and superior worth of the ordinary people. In societies undergoing rapid transition, with blurred images and conflicting goals, the situation is especially propitious for the growth of these contra-cultural configurations. A subculture of youth develops as a secretive autonomous entity. It represents, often, the combined pull of revolution and of cloak-and-dagger adventure. A sense of insecurity and frustration, tacit encouragement and support by vested interests, and legitimation of its activities by strong in-group solidarity contribute to the persistence of such entities. In certain situations youth culture functions as a caricature of adult culture. The contemporary youth cultures of India correspond to these patterns, which have fairly wide cross-cultural occurrence.

That India would have a problem of troubled youth could be anticipated. What should really worry us now is our inability to hold it in check. The lapses of youth have at least a psychological explanation, but the failures of the elders are more serious and call for deep heart-searching.

Many attempts have been made to diagnose this rebelliousness and to isolate the factors responsible for it. Some attribute it to faulty socialization, especially to authoritarian fathers who seek to impose a rigid discipline which is far beyond the capability of their children. But several preceding generations of children have had to go through the same process, and their reactions never attained the scale or the intensity of the present-day revolt. One wonders if the Spocks are right, and if their doctrines of permissiveness deserve the uncritical acceptance they have received. The dysfunctional aspects of permissiveness must also be understood. The inter-generation gap explains much more, but not all. Today it does involve sharp structural discontinuities and simultaneous participation in conflicting cultural worlds. This creates considerable stress. But the gap is, in many significant aspects, man-made, and its imbalances can be corrected.

An international style of protest and revolt has developed during the last decade, and its echo is heard in India as well. Admittedly some of the protest in India is imitative, but this fact alone cannot explain the pervasiveness of the discontent.

It should be admitted that India was not adequately prepared for the educational explosion and its attendant problems. The special requirements of the new kinds of students that poured into our colleges and universities were neither anticipated nor attended to. The academic routine of the universities offered little challenge or stimulation to the growing number of students. Teacher-student contact was minimal; in fact, their distance and isolation was increasing. In the name of tradition, outmoded procedures were sought to be perpetuated, but no attempt was made to rectify the structural incompatibilities of the system. The temples of learning were themselves the scene of fierce in-fighting. Notable exceptions apart, the faculty and the top administration failed to set an example either of character or of performance. What is worse, they even sought to manipulate student power to further their own interests. This had to be, because too many convenient mediocrities—and even lesser beings—came to occupy the once exalted office of Vice-Chancellor, and faculty positions and promotions came under the umbrella of political patronage. Many political parties could not resist the temptation of fishing in the troubled waters of the universities. But their attitude to student activists was, and remains, ambivalent.

In the final analysis, it is difficult to isolate the students from the rest of the community. The collapse of the general normative structure, the low ideological articulation, and the growing sense of frustration in the country have all contributed to the ferment in the colleges and the universities.

The youth need a vision of the future. The credibility gap between the elders and the young has to be reduced. For this the leaders of the system must visibly demonstrate that they mean what they say. The establishment should be able to convince the youth that it is sensitive and responsive to dissent, that changes can be worked out within the system, and that it can cleanse itself of the hypocrisy and cant at which the blistering fire of the youth is directed. Above all, the young will have to be persuaded that the ballot box can be a more potent means of bringing about change than the barrel of a gun.

ELEVEN

Religion in a Secular Society

With pardonable anthropocentrism man can make a well-founded claim to uniqueness. His unparalleled capacity to symbolize marks him out from all other members of the animal kingdom. Endowed with a reasoning mind, an algebraic mentality, and the faculty of articulate speech, he has been able to build an elaborate and complex symbol system that permeates his cultural universe. *Homo sapiens* has a rich and varied cultural inventory because quite early in his evolutionary career he refused to accept the given order: he began to question, to doubt, to deny, to speculate, to explore, and to experiment. In consequence, his cognitive map was progressively enlarged. Through his unceasing search and speculation he learned to manipulate his environment, and succeeded in creating cultural worlds whose complexity grows with every major advancement in knowledge. As a tool-maker he excelled himself, and it is a tribute to his capacity to wield symbols that he has built a truly remarkable material culture. Symbols played an equally important part in shaping the patterns of his belief and his social organization; in time they also acquired an extraordinary range and variety. But changes in the scheme of social organization and in cultural values did not often keep pace with advancements in knowledge. This absence of fit between the socio-cultural order and the intellectual-technological order resulted in imbalances and disharmonies. Because of his attachment to the past, in some areas of life he could not respond adequately to the challenges of the present and of the future. He has had to strike a balance between continuity and change and this has not always been easy.

At different stages of his social evolution, different factors provided the bases of solidarity. Ethnic origin, race, religion, national identity, language, and ideology have, at different stages, constituted the principal bases of cohesion. Each in its time was invested with a mystique, and each acquired a dominating symbolic value. With the passage of time, consequent on changes in the technological, social, and psychological environment, they lost or gained their commanding position, but in the contemporary cultural landscape each one of them asserts itself in one form or other in different settings. In the rational perspective of modernity, whose idiom and ethos emanate from science, the free play of these parochial and constrictive forces looks amazing; unpalatable though they may be, they have to be accepted as facts of life.

Let us consider the case of religion. Of all living animals man alone prays. No other creature has a scheme of psychic satisfactions that partially replaces the need for biological satisfactions. Man's cultural world embodies also a conception of the mysterious unknown. He has different systems of beliefs and practices, embodying the idea of a supernatural power and of personified supernatural forces that formalize the conception of the relation between man and his environment. This is religion.

Beliefs constitute the cognitive part of religion: rituals represent its expressive and instrumental aspects. Through them the individual and his group acquire a system of meanings and motivations. Religion is a symbolic statement of the social order—the metaphor for society itself.

Religion played—and continues to play—a key role in the affairs of man and society because of its functions. Several of these functions can be identified. Perhaps the most important is its *explanatory function.* To the *why*, the *who*, the *what*, the *where*, and the *wheretofore* relating to the mysterious tremendum, religion offers answers and explanations. Second, religion has an *integrative function.* It provides support amid uncertainty; consolation amid failure, frustration, and disappointment; and reconciliation amid alienation from goals and norms. Closely related to this is the third function of religion, which may be called the *identity function.* It provides a basis for the maintenance of a transcendental relationship that makes for security and a firm identity. Fourth, it has a *validating function.* It provides moral justification and powerful sanctions to all basic institutions, values, and goals. Fifth, by enforcing conformity and by holding in check various forms of deviance, it performs an important *control function.*

Sixth, by providing for the reduction and/or satisfaction of painful drives, it performs an *expressive function.* To these can be added the *prophetic function*, expressed in protest against established forms and conditions; the *maturation function* providing recognition and cushioning at critical turns in an individual's life through *rites de passage*; and the *wishfulfilment function*, covering both latent and manifest wishes.

As the area of scientific knowledge and technology widens, the area of religion shrinks. Some of its functions are taken over by other agencies. The strength of its hold and the range of its influence are greater in simpler and technologically less developed societies. Such societies also have the need to know—may it be even incorrectly. Although they have a body of empirical knowledge, in several fields of life it is much too inadequate. Where experience and empirical knowledge fail, religion offers the answers. In societies with a scientific ethos the range of these explanations is narrowed, and they are less implicitly believed. But in technologically less developed societies, lacking rational cause-effect explanations, rituals and symbolic acts are employed on a wide scale to placate supernatural powers for immediate and worldly gain. The collective and the communal aspects of worship are more important in these societies. In modern industrial societies the hold of religious belief over different aspects of life declines, although interest in religion as a phenomenon persists. It sheds much of its collective and communal overtones and becomes largely a personal concern.

The process of secularization starts when institutions of society in different functional areas resist subservience to established religion and gain a measure of autonomy. In the process, the institutions and functionaries of religion lose their control over several fields of social activity such as politics, diplomacy, economics and trade, education, medicine, and so on. This marks the ascendancy of civil authority. Many of the traditional functions of religion are taken care of by secular institutions. Even in the religious sphere, dissent is tolerated: understanding and accommodation emerge as the principal themes governing inter-religious group behaviour. A religious world view, in which the entire framework of action has a religious orientation, undergoes a thorough modification. Sources of cognition, motivation, and sanctions get diversified. Religion does not remain the sole—or even the most important—agency from which social values, goals, and norms of action emanate. By adopting rational and scientific procedures, the secular society chalks out alternative paths of social action. When necessary, it resists uncalled for interference from religious authority.

In some societies, secularization has been attained through a long evolutionary process. Compulsions inherent in the processes of technological change and economic growth necessitated the redefinition of the role of religion and the delimitation of the sphere of its authority. With the growth of a temper of science, religion lost its pervasive influence. Interdenominational conflicts were tempered by emerging norms of tolerance. To a great extent, the acceptance of religious doctrine became a matter of individual choice. The central values of religion survived, but many of the associated myths and rituals suffered a gradual eclipse.

The situation in many developing societies, however, is different. They have gone secular by legislative fiats. In truth they lack the infrastructure for the emergence of true secularism. The modern institutional framework they have adopted is limited in its reach and in its penetration. They do not as yet have diversified institutions that can effectively perform the traditional functions of religion. These societies remain affective, particularistic, and communal. In them, religion often emerges as a political factor. Bigotry and intolerance, deriving more from superstition than from the basic premises of any religion, continue.

Ironically, these are the societies that need secularism most if their visions of prosperity are to materialize. A sense of nationness among the people is one of the preconditions of development, but the fibre of nationhood in these societies is fragile. Inter-religious tensions and conflicts come in the way of true national cohesion. Problems are viewed in a narrow and communal, rather than in a wide and national, perspective. The emergence of positive and forward-looking attitudes is blocked by excessive absorption in rituals and by uncritical acceptance of a dated world view. Religious orientations shape attitudes to work, wealth, and happiness, and hinder the growth of an ethic that would be conducive to progress. Secularization is thus doubly indicated for these societies—to curb the divisiveness that springs from religious differences, and to clear the way for the emergence of a structural-motivational framework suited to rapid development.

Of course, no society is completely secular, nor are all the basic teachings of religion dysfunctional. Many characteristic attitudes, dispositions, values, and cultural orientations that emanate from religious traditions are worth preserving. A secular society would not reject them offhand. Religion has inspired and stimulated a significantly large number of conspicuous creations in fields as diverse as art, architecture, literature, philosophy, and music. All these will continue to be cherished as high-water marks of man's creative endeavour. But religion will have to adapt itself to the changing ethos. The professed finality of the words of prophets or of the prescriptions of sacred books notwithstanding, all religions have made situational adjustments and compromises. No religion has been able to preserve its original social forms and cultural patterns in their pristine purity, and to meet the challenges of the contemporary world, it will have to accept necessary modifications. Insofar as it promotes detached goodwill and disinterested commitment, religion would be functional to the aims of modernization. But, if it goes counter to the emerging conceptions of the dignity of the human individual and to the canons of distributive justice, both its content and its form will have to be modified.

Men—some men, at any rate—will continue to need faith. They would need support during traumatic experiences and extreme distress. To them, religion will remain a necessity. In fact, until science can provide all the answers, religion will continue to illuminate some of the imponderables of the universe. On a higher spiritual and moral plane, religion is not necessarily inconsistent with the idiom of science and the ethos of progress. A secular and modern society is not against religion as such, but it has to fight superstition and intolerance as well as bigotry and obscurantism. Separate religious identities are permissible so long as they do not question the legitimacy of larger national boundaries. If religion does not bar the emergence of a national consensus on the goals of social action, inhibit national integration, and obstruct the adaptation of society to the fast changing world, it can be left undisturbed. Under these conditions, diversity is to be welcomed. Areas of personal beliefs that are not inconsistent with the larger needs of society can be upheld and protected by society. But beliefs and practices that bring about discord and disharmony between different religious groups will require resolute action. Inter-religious harmony and consensus for progress would be an acceptable and attractive slogan for a secular society oriented to modernity.

TWELVE

Sociological Implications of Secularism

From the beginning of his social life man has sought certain bases of identification and has tended to distinguish sharply between "in group" and "out group". Having settled on a criterion, he invests fantastic loyalty into it and relentlessly promotes and defends it as a matter of honour and pride. With the gradual extension of man's social universe the limits of "we groups" have widened considerably; from kin-based units like family and lineage to the nation state, through several intermediate stages, he has indeed travelled a long way. Tribal totems, common ethnic origin, linguistic affinity, class consciousness, and religion have all been rallying points and motivating forces for human groups in different periods of man's history. Over the centuries some old symbols have lost vitality and new ones have gained ascendancy. But in many developing societies of the contemporary world, several centuries appear to coexist. Many diverse bonds of cohesion operate with equal force to draw the allegiance of different segments of the population. Where the fibre of nationhood has not toughened sufficiently, these contrary pulls—operating at different levels and at different times in different contexts—present baffling contradictions and pose puzzling problems. Perhaps the worst hit among them are the multi-ethnic, multi-lingual, and multi-religious societies.

Consider the case of India—an old society but a new nation. Behind the country's facade of national unity lurk a bewildering variety of parochial loyalties that defiantly raise their ugly heads from time to time. Tribalism, linguism and, above all, religious communalism are hard and painful facts of life with us. They have persisted during the last two decades with a singular tenacity, with all too brief periods of relief. We can ignore them only at our own peril.

In the politics of pre-partition India the Hindu versus Muslim perspective significantly coloured the political processes of the country. Interests such as the attainment of freedom and the eradiction of poverty and backwardness were manifestly or latently viewed in a framework provided by this distorted perspective. Even today the wall of distrust and suspicion has not been demolished. Provisions of the constitution and ideological professions from political platforms to the contrary, this wall still exists. Myopic policies focused on short-run political gains have nursed the suspicion and have, in a way, guarded the gulf that separates the two major communities. The gulf may not have widened, but it has not been narrowed either. The other religious and cultural minorities, though less articulate and vocal, also have not always felt secure and have faintly (and sometimes even assertively) voiced their misgivings.

The approach to the problem, in India, is basically sound on the theoretical level. In the socio-cultural sphere, there is no insistence on the imposition—or on the emergence—of a rigidly uniform pattern: stabilized cultural pluralism appears to be the desired objective.

Religious faith and worship are matters of individual conscience, and every citizen is free to profess his religion. Understanding and tolerance—sought to be consciously promoted—are expected to reduce the areas and occasions of conflict. The State has equal respect for all religions, but is at the same time equidistant from them all. In mundane matters, in respect of all citizens, it is to be guided by rational criteria; religious considerations are not to colour its economic, social, or political policies.

National integration is to be achieved in terms of specific interests, articulated as a series of national goals which are to be attained at different stages in the foreseeable future. The twin processes of problem identification and problem solution are to be Indianized; in other words, they are to be viewed and handled in a national perspective.

But these laudable policies do not seem to click. One wonders why. We are all set to move fast on the road leading to communal amity and secularization. Indeed, there is a great deal of commotion without much motion.

The hangover from the past has left several mental barriers. The minorities are in fear of the giant majority, which has the brute strength to overpower them and divert them of their distinctive characteristics. This psychological fear has its roots in the past and goes back to the era in which the two-nation theory was preached on this very premise. The majority—on its part—views with distrust the separatist overtones discernible in some aspects of minority politics. To many, the extraterritorial loyalties—overt and covert, real or imaginary—of some sections of some minorities are a source of worry and annoyance. Deep-seated attitude patterns and ways of thinking persist.

Perhaps the minority does not see any evidence of the magnanimity that is expected of the majority in the new order. Also, a section of the majority, perhaps, does not notice any appreciable change in the political strategies of the more significant and vocal minorities. Both continue to think along pre-independence grooves. Psychological stereotypes do not adequately reflect the pragmatic adjustments that have already taken place. The mischief lies in their being able to take sudden hold over the minds of people in periods of stress, and thus to partially unsettle the process of stabilization.

The powerful move towards modernization notwithstanding, the fundamental postulates and the basic framework of Indian society have not yet undergone a radical change. Status evaluation is still largely ascriptive. A person is judged by a series of qualities believed to be inherited by him, rather than by his performance. Loyalties continue to be particularistic rather than universalistic. Kin and caste, region and religion, thus, get allegiance that should otherwise have gone to universal principles and to a national perspective. This helps in the maintenance of a closed segmentary social system and blocks the emergence of an open system based on loyalty to universal criteria. Religious emphases and attachment to ritual forms bar the emergence of secular ends-means criteria based on rationality. This social situation does not stimulate empathy—the capacity to see things as others see them. Empathy is a precondition of inter-group adjustment and harmony.

In social structure there is some evidence of relaxation of rigidity, and of a little more mobility, but not enough. The structural distance between major religions and cultural minorities has not been reduced significantly. Factors inhibiting free interchange and participation among them are still strong.

The economics of scarcity, by restricting adequate allocation of resources, sows seeds of tension and discord. The competitive politics of an immature democracy encourages recruitment and mobilization on every possible basis of identification and allegiance irrespective of their injurious long-term effects. There are notable exceptions, but a realistic target oriented strategy leaves little scope for a different political approach. The absence of consensus, and of a minimal code of ethics, in this field contribute to the prevailing state of affairs.

Charters and constitutions, democratic governmental frameworks and institutions, and professional affirmation of faith are important, but the men behind them are infinitely more so. Few governments have been able to legislate fully the patterns of inter-group relations for its people. Law can be a valuable step in removing difficulties and hardships faced by particular groups. It can also, theoretically, open up new opportunities. But the actual removal of hardships and the access to opportunity would depend, in a large measure, upon the mental preparedness and emotional responses of the people.

With out adequate institutional change one cannot visualize the emergence of new images and attitudes. In their absence one often finds a gap between profession and practice, and between formal structure and actual behaviour. The situation is sometimes complicated by the creation of new aspirations without any provision of avenues for their realization.

True secularism is a style of thought and a way of life. The magic of words—either on the platform or in the law book—cannot produce instant secularization of outlook, values, and behaviour patterns. Secularization presuppose deep and thorough-going psychological transformations which, in their turn, are dependent on institutional change. Admonitions and exhortations are at best instruments of limited utility. Unaccompanied by substantial social change and massive educational support, they can attain little.

The secular mind is characterized by rationality, empathy and psychic mobility. It calculates on rational ends-means bases. It stipulates strategies on a wide canvas. These attributes can thrive best in an open society. They are sustained by a cultural ethos of inter-group understanding and cooperation. To reorder group allegiances and to restructure their patterns of interaction a larger national identity, rooted in interests, is essential. This feat of social engineering will require a socio-economic and political system that can interlink and interpenetrate various sub-cultural groups. The payoff of prejudice and parochialism must first be reduced and ultimately eliminated. The gains of interdependence and cooperation should be visibly demonstrated. Secular ideology alone can achieve little. Accompanied by adequate and constructive action on the economic and political fronts, it can be a prime mover of change.

To many, democracy is government by discussion. Ideas, if they are perceptively and imaginatively projected, can meaningfully influence the course of history. We need to bring into the situation a greater sense of realism and also, if I may say so, a little sense of humour. The absurdity and futility of the recurrent communal approach have to be brought home forcefully.

Index

Index

Index